GARDENING
——WITH——
ROSES

A Practical and Inspirational Guide

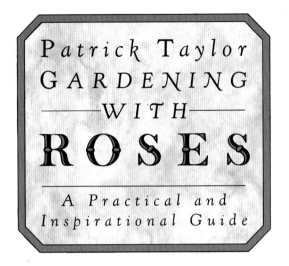

Patrick Taylor
GARDENING
——WITH——
ROSES

A Practical and
Inspirational Guide

Timber Press
Portland, Oregon

DEDICATION
For Sophie, with much love

First published in 1995 by
PAVILION BOOKS LTD
26 Upper Ground, London SE1 9PD

Text copyright © 1995 Patrick Taylor

Illustrations copyright © 1995 Open Books Publishing Ltd

This book was devised and produced by
Open Books Publishing Ltd, Beaumont House
Wells BA5 2LD, Somerset, UK

Designer: Andrew Barron,
Andrew Barron and Collis Clements Associates

Computer Consultant: Mike Mepham

A CIP catalogue record for this book is available from the British
Library

ISBN: 1-85793-420-2

Printed and Bound in Hong Kong by
Mandarin Offset

First published in North America by
Timber Press Inc
133 S.W. Second Avenue, Suite 450,
Portland, Oregon 97204-3527, U.S.A.

ISBN: 0-88192-286-2

CONTENTS

❧

Acknowledgements	7
INTRODUCTION	9
BUSH ROSES	37
CLIMBING ROSES	185
Roses by Category (colour, foliage and scent)	242
Roses for Shade	246
Roses for Informal Places and for Structure	248
Reading List	249
Hardiness Zones	250
Index	252

ACKNOWLEDGEMENTS

The research for this book took me into some of the finest gardens of the day and wherever I went I was given the friendly help and generous hospitality that seems to be typical of gardeners. In particular I should like to thank the following: Amanda Beales (Peter Beales Roses), Mr and Mrs A.H. Chambers (Kiftsgate Court), Mr and Mrs Charles Hornby (Hodges Barn), Sheila Little (Claverton Manor), Lady Anne Rasch and Gwyn Perry (Head Gardener) (Heale House), Lord and Lady Saye and Sele, and Chris Hopkins (Head Gardener) (Broughton Castle), David Stone (Head Gardener, Mottisfont Abbey), Lord and Lady Tollemache (Helmingham Hall); and the gardening staff of David Austin Roses (in particular Mrs Olwen Gaut); of La Bagatelle in Paris; of Mannington Hall (Norfolk); of La Roseraie de l'Haÿ-les-Roses; and of the Gardens of the Rose (St Albans). I am very grateful to Dr Tony Lord who has saved me, yet again, from some nasty mistakes.

The National Trust gave me much help, in particular the permission to photograph in the great rose garden at Mottisfont Abbey for which I thank them most warmly.

My wife Caroline, once again, immensely improved my text and I am profoundly grateful to her. Andrew Barron of Andrew Barron and Collis Clements Associates designed the book with his usual skill and valuable interest. Colin Webb and his colleagues at Pavilion Books have been as helpful and agreeable to deal with as ever.

All the photographs were taken by myself. I have tried to show the roses as naturally as possible; that is to say, I have resorted to no 'art direction'. If there are patches of mildew or black spot, dead or discoloured flowers, then that, I am sorry to say, is in the nature of the plants.

Patrick Taylor
Wells, Somerset

INTRODUCTION

───────── ❧ ─────────

For many gardeners and garden visitors the greatest pleasure of the year comes from the garden in high summer, when the air is heady with the scent of roses. Roses are exceptionally versatile plants, and in this book I have chosen those that I think are particularly successful for a variety of uses in the garden: for formal beds, high walls, containers, hedges, mixed borders or the long grass of an orchard. The qualities I have sought are beauty and character of flower, scent, foliage and habit; and also (perhaps the most precious quality of all), the ability to harmonise with other plantings and make a vital contribution to the atmosphere of the garden as a whole.

In the past roses were often segregated in a rose garden well away from the house, and not visited out of season. The gardener today prefers to use them in conjunction with other plants and in relation to the house, which puts an emphasis on the ease with which the roses associate with other plants.

This is a personal choice, but in describing the individual nature of each rose I try to explain why I like it and what makes it, in my opinion, a good garden plant. On the whole I have found the qualities I sought in the old roses, or in those which have been bred recently in that tradition. The very fact that so many of the early cultivars survive in cultivation today indicates that they possess some quality that is especially admired. Too many of the most recent roses seem to me appallingly ugly and, above all, very bad mixers, though there have been some brilliant successes from modern rose breeders; any gardener, for example, will find plants to admire among the roses of the Kordes family in Germany or of David Austin in England.

Most of my examples flower only once, in June. I do not regard this as a shortcoming; in many cases the fleeting beauty of a garden plant is one of its charms. However, I have not forgotten the needs of those owners of small gardens who have room for only a few roses. They require varieties that flower repeatedly, have good scent, beautiful foliage and, if possible, decorative fruit.

In this chapter I look briefly at the history and classification of roses, and then talk in general terms about their cultivation and best use in the garden, as well as about the type of plants that associate well with them. In the 'Rose Directory' – the heart of the book – I describe in detail the particular qualities of each rose, and give more specific suggestions about its use and about good association planting. My hope is that the text, supported in most instances by a colour photograph, will not only help you in your choice of roses for your garden, but also how to use them to their best advantage.

The History of Roses

Wild roses are found only in the Northern Hemisphere, most frequently in its temperate regions; between 100 and 150 species exist. They are members of the family Rosaceae, which includes several fruit trees – apples, pears and plums among them – and valuable garden plants such as alchemillas, cotoneasters, crataegus, potentillas, sorbus, spiraea and many others.

From very early on the rose was held in special esteem. Classical literature and mythology are full of references to it. In the Christian era the rose was adopted as a moral symbol: the desirable object which could be achieved only by braving the thorns; its basic five petals symbolising the five senses which had to be subjugated in order to arrive at the spiritual goal. The rose also became the symbol of the Virgin Mary and is

Rosa 'Great Maiden's Blush' – one of the oldest garden roses, dating back to at least the 15th century

depicted in those delightful 15th-century Flemish miniatures of the Virgin in her enclosed garden, which are among the earliest pictures of gardens in the West.

Although the rose was studied by botanists from quite early on, certainly by the Romans, and one or two kinds, such as *Rosa gallica* var. *officinalis*, appear in gardens before the Renaissance, it is not until the second half of the 18th century that roses were widely used. In 1744 an English nursery, Lee & Kennedy, describe forty-four roses in their catalogue. Later, the Empress Josephine, a customer of Lee & Kennedy, did much to make roses fashionable; by the time of her death in 1814 she had collected over 250 varieties for the garden at La Malmaison.

The 19th century saw an explosion in the popularity of roses, and in the breeding of new varieties. In England the nursery of Paul & Son in Hertfordshire, established in 1806, launched a stream of garden-worthy roses, many of which are still in cultivation, including 'Goldfinch', 'Mermaid' and 'Paul's Scarlet'. In France Antoine Jacques, head gardener to the Duc d'Orléans, bred several good varieties in the 1820s, such as 'Adélaïde d'Orléans' and 'Félicité Perpétue', and France remained at the centre of rose breeding throughout the 19th century. The German firm of Kordes Söhne was founded in 1887 and introduced many excellent roses, such as 'Iceberg', 'Max Graf' and the 'Frühlings' series. It is still very active.

Throughout the 20th century new roses have continued to pour forth. Today, although at least 1,500 varieties of rose are grown commercially, many will survive in cultivation even more briefly than the ephemeral figures they often commemorate.

The Classification of Roses

Almost all cultivars of roses used in gardens today arise from an immensely complicated hodge-podge of genetic influences. Although roses are grouped according to their general features – Gallicas, Albas and so on – these fairly arbitrary divisions become very blurred at the edges. For example, only one of the groups, the Gallicas, is derived from a single surviving wild rose, *Rosa gallica*, and even here there has been much hybridisation with roses from other groups. And there is clear genetic evidence of the influence of Gallicas on Bourbons, Damasks, Hybrid Perpetuals and Hybrid Teas. Indeed, the same rose may be assigned by different authorities to different groups, while many 20th-century roses, for example some of those bred by Kordes and Austin, belong to none.

However, most roses within each group do share more or less distinct family resemblances, and I have given the name of the group for each rose. At the very least the classification provides a practical way of referring to different pruning needs.

Alba

Alba roses are derived from a hybrid, *Rosa × alba*, which was probably a cross between the European native dog rose, *R. canina*, and the Damask rose, *R. × damascena*, an ancient garden hybrid. The characteristic Alba is a strong-growing, strikingly upright bush with beautiful grey-green foliage. Some will exceed 8ft/2.5m in height and are among the tallest garden varieties. The flowers are usually double and are limited in colour to white or pink. Typical Albas among those that I describe in this book are the

A typical Bourbon rose:
Rosa 'Boule de Neige'

'Jacobite Rose' (*R.* × *alba* 'Alba Maxima'), 'Great Maiden's Blush', 'Königin von Dänemark' and 'Madame Plantier'.

Bourbon

The Bourbon roses owe their origins to a chance hybrid on the Ile de Bourbon (now called Réunion) in the Indian Ocean, between *Rosa* × *pallida* 'Odorata' (formerly known as 'Old Blush China') and the old Damask *R.* × *damascena semperflorens* – known, because of its ability to flower more than once, as the 'Autumn Damask'. This was the first known hybrid of a rose from China crossed with one from the West. The result was a rose with large double flowers, delicious scent and vigorous growth; it had the additional virtue of repeat flowering. Among those that I describe are 'Boule de Neige', 'Madame Isaac Pereire' and the Climber 'Zéphirine Drouhin'. Even those classed as bushes often have rather lax growth and may be trained as climbers.

Buds and flower of the Centifolia *Rosa* 'Fantin-Latour'

Centifolia

The Centifolias go back at least to the 17th century when they were often shown in Dutch still-life paintings. They are bush roses and as their name suggests they have double flowers, often exceptionally well scented. Many old Centifolias survive in cultivation; among those that I include here are 'De Meaux', 'Fantin-Latour', 'Petite de Hollande' and 'Robert le Diable'.

China Roses

China Roses are all descended from introductions from China to the West in the late 18th century. They may be bush or climbing roses and they have in common a delicacy of growth and flower, and repeat flowering. They are among the more tender roses, needing protection in a warm garden. Indeed, some are best grown in pots, kept indoors in winter and brought out to enjoy the sun in a sheltered spot during the summer. Among the Chinas described in this book are

'Hermosa', *R. × odorata* 'Mutabilis' and *R. × odorata* 'Pallida'.

Climbing
These are a jumble of roses, not so vigorous nor so lax in habit as Ramblers, but nonetheless possessed of the climbing urge. Among those that I include here are 'Céline Forestier', 'City of York' and 'Constance Spry'.

Damask
Damask roses take their name from the ancient hybrid, *Rosa × damascena*, known since the 16th century. Modern Damask roses owe their repeat flowering to a particular form, *R. × damascena semperflorens*. They are medium-sized shrubs, rarely exceeding 5ft/1.5m in height, and their flowers are typically double and white or pink in colour. Almost all are very well scented. I include, among others, 'Belle Amour', 'Celsiana' and 'Madame Hardy'.

Floribunda
This group, also known as Cluster-flowered, consists of modern bush roses, all of which are perpetual-flowering and carry their flowers in many-stemmed clusters. They vary immensely in every other way. Among those that I have included are 'Gruss an Aachen', 'Iceberg' and 'White Pet'.

Gallica
Rosa gallica is a wild rose found widely in Europe. It has rather large single flowers, up to 3 1/2in/9cm across, deep pink fading towards white in the centre. Its leaves are attractively pleated and curved, with finely toothed edges, and it forms an upright bush with very fine thorns. It gave rise to one of the oldest surviving garden cultivars, *R. gallica* 'Versicolor', known also as 'Rosa Mundi', which was described in 1583 by the botanist Clusius. Almost all Gallicas found today are French 19th-century cultivars; the Empress Josephine is said to have had 160 varieties at La

Illustration opposite: The Damask *Rosa* 'Belle Amour'

Malmaison. Among others described in this book are 'Assemblage des Beautés', 'Belle de Crécy', 'Camaïeux', 'Charles de Mills' and 'Tuscany Superb'. The characteristic flower colour of the Gallicas ranges from pink to the deepest maroon. The form of the flower is rather flat and many of them are double. None has white flowers. Some of the Gallicas have rather spindly lax growth deriving from influences other than *R. gallica*. They flower once only in the summer.

Hybrid Musk

The Hybrid Musks are unusual among rose groups in that they were the creation of a single breeder, the Englishman Joseph Pemberton, in the early 20th century. One of his sources was the rose 'Trier', bred by the German nurseryman Peter Lambert in 1904. As a group the Hybrid Musks have in common excellent scent and the ability to flower throughout the season. In this book I describe, among others, 'Buff Beauty', 'Cornelia', 'Felicia' and 'Penelope'.

Hybrid Perpetual

The Hybrid Perpetuals date from the middle of the 19th century when rose breeders succeeded in breeding a new kind of rose that would flower repeatedly after its first flowering in June. Many of these introductions are still to be found in gardens today. Many different roses were involved, but the strain that gave them their perpetual-flowering characteristic was the China rose. Although the Hybrid Perpetuals are bush roses some grow very lanky and make better climbers. In the past the classic way of growing Hybrid Perpetuals was to peg down the lax new growth which encourages flowers on side shoots. Among those described in this book are 'Baron Girod de l'Ain', 'Baronne Prévost', 'Le Havre' and 'Souvenir du Docteur Jamain'.

Hybrid Tea

Hybrid Teas were introduced in the late 19th century and are the most widely seen group of roses. They tend

to have large flowers in every imaginable colour, bold foliage and will flower throughout the season. Most are bush roses but a few have produced climbing sports. Among the Hybrid Teas described in this book are 'Etoile de Hollande', 'Lady Waterlow', 'Madame Caroline Testout' and 'Mrs Herbert Stevens'.

Moss

The curious Moss roses came from a cultivar of the Provence Rose, *Rosa × centifolia*, a garden hybrid going back to the 16th century. 'Old Pink Moss', *R. × centifolia* 'Muscosa', known since 1700 and one of the oldest surviving rose cultivars, has strange moss-like growth on stems and flower buds. Some of the Mosses I describe are *R. × centifolia* 'Cristata', 'Madame Delaroche-Lambert', 'Nuits de Young' and 'Salet'. Apart from the mossy growth, they all produce double flowers in colours ranging from white to the deepest crimson. Some are recurrent-flowering.

Noisette

The Noisette roses were evolved in the early 19th century by the North American nurseryman Philippe Noisette of Charleston, South Carolina. They include both bushes and climbers. Among them are the climbers 'Blush Noisette', 'Claire Jacquier' and 'Madame Alfred Carrière'. All are very sweetly scented and repeat-flower well.

Polyantha

Polyantha roses date from the late 19th century. They are bushes, with the occasional climbing sport, perpetual-flowering but notably lacking in scent. Polyantha roses described in this book include 'Cécile Brunner', 'Mevrouw Nathalie Nypels' and 'Iceberg'.

Portland

Portland roses go back to the beginning of the 19th century. With much influence from *Rosa gallica*, they are medium to small bushes, often with well scented

A typical Portland rose: *Rosa* 'Marchesa Boccella'

flowers and often recurrent-flowering. Among the Portlands described in this book are 'Comte de Chambord', 'Marchesa Boccella' and *R.* 'Portlandica'.

Rambler
Rambler roses are all very vigorous, putting out long flexible shoots, and are normally grown as climbers. Many of them derive from East Asian species. Among the Ramblers I describe are 'Albéric Barbier', 'Albertine', 'Phyllis Bide' and 'Sanders' White'.

Species Roses
The wild roses provide some of the most beautiful, and problem-free, garden plants. I include in this book *Rosa bracteata*, *R. glauca*, *R. moyesii*, *R. villosa* and several others. Many roses bred by Kordes, particularly the 'Frühlings' series, have the character of species roses, both in appearance and disease resistance.

Tea
The Tea roses date date from the 19th century when a Bourbon rose was crossed with a China rose, 'Hume's Blush Pink'. They are both bush and climbing roses, often with large flowers and delicious scent. Among those described here are 'Gloire de Dijon', 'Lady Hillingdon, Climbing' and 'Sombreuil, Climbing'.

The Cultivation of Roses

Few gardens possess the perfect conditions so confidently recommended in books for growing roses! Good circulation of air, well drained fertile soil, plenty of light, no extreme of acidity or alkalinity – all these are counsels of perfection that will be hard to meet. Furthermore, most gardeners will also want to grow other plants, which may need different conditions from those prescribed for roses. Many gardeners will have seen, sometimes in their own gardens, magnificent roses, in perfect floriferous health, that have been planted with very little care and thought. But a little care is not hard to give and will in the long run produce much better roses. This is a very large subject and all I can do here is make a few suggestions.

Roses come container-grown at any time of the year, or may be ordered bare-rooted from nurseries in winter. The hole that you dig for a new rose should be 18in/45cm in diameter and about half as deep – just deep enough to accommodate the roots, which usually grow to one side rather than straight down. Break up the soil at the bottom of the hole. If the rose is grafted, the union between plant and rootstock should be exactly at ground level or very slightly below. Spread out the roots and fill in with fine compost-rich soil, adding bonemeal (half a handful per rose is quite enough) and a certain amount of grit to encourage root growth. Give the plant a little shake from time to time as you fill the hole, to help the soil to fall down and surround the roots. Firm the soil by treading it down.

It is possible to plant a containerised rose at any time of the year but it will be easier to plant, and make a better start, if you plant it, as you would a bare-rooted rose, when it is dormant. Plant it when the soil is neither waterlogged nor frosted, and soak the roots of both containerised and bare-rooted plants before planting. It is unwise to plant a new rose where there was a rose before without taking precautions. The new rose may otherwise suffer from 'rose sickness', caused by a build-up of infections to which roses are especially susceptible. To protect the new rose, a substantial quantity of the old soil, at least 24in/60cm cubic volume should either be sterilised or replaced with fresh soil.

A one-year-old plant should be pruned very hard after planting – reducing growth to 2in/5cm. Most containerised plants are a minimum of two years old and strong shoots should be cut back to 4in/10cm, and weaker shoots to 2in/5cm. Climbing roses trained on a wall should be planted at least 12in/30cm away from the wall so that their roots do not suffer from drought.

Once the rose is established it will benefit from regular feeding. Repeat- or perpetual-flowering roses in particular need plenty of nourishment. In early spring a deep mulch of the best compost you can lay your hands on, with bonemeal raked in underneath, is a good start. In a mixed border roses will be competing for nourishment with many other plants and to perform really well must be copiously fed. Foliar feeding is a convenient way of supplying nourishment but do not continue feeding after peak flowering is reached. This will promote excessive soft growth that may be vulnerable to hard early frosts.

Diseases

The subject of disease is one too large to cope with adequately in this book. Some gardeners spray their roses weekly throughout the season. Others, myself included, are nervous of using too many chemicals in the garden and take the view that the roses will have to look after themselves. A vigorous, well-fed and well cared for plant will be much less susceptible to disease. I have had roses blighted with mildew and black-spot but these things come and go, and although the leaves may become unsightly it does not appear to affect flowering and I cannot remember any rose in my garden dying.

Pruning

Pruning is a subject that some gardeners find deeply absorbing, and it can be made to seem as simple, or as

The art of pruning and training as practised at La Roseraie de l'Haÿ

'Paul's Scarlet Pillar' beautifully trained and pruned in the Parc de la Tête d'Or at Lyon

complicated, as you like. The single most important thing is to understand the purpose of pruning at all. In nature, after all, roses do not get pruned, so why should you do it? There are four chief reasons for pruning roses in the garden: the first, deadheading – the removal of dead flowers in repeat-flowering roses – is to encourage the appearance of further flowers; the second, the removal of weak or unproductive growth to the base of the plant, or the cutting back of strong growth, is to encourage vigorous new flower-bearing growth the following year; the third, the removal of unsightly dead or damaged wood, is to tidy up the plant and prevent disease; and the fourth, thinning, shaping or reducing the rose, is to improve its appearance.

Pruning manuals have diagrams illustrating the perfect angle and position of the cut, immediately above an outward-pointing bud or shoot. But every gardener will have experienced difficulty in finding this outward-pointing bud just where they feel the cut should be made. Furthermore, a recent experiment has shown that bush roses pruned with a hedgetrimmer performed just as well as those meticulously hand-pruned according to the classic rules.

The first thing to decide is whether or not a particular rose needs pruning at all. The best guide is the character of the plant. Species roses, for example, or those like the 'Frühlings' group that resemble wild roses, derive much of their beauty from their natural grace and habit of growth. That is an absolutely overriding consideration, and pruning should be limited to the removal of dead or damaged growth. Furthermore, such roses also have very decorative hips, which would be lost if the plant were pruned.

As for deciding when to prune, the single most important factor is whether the rose produces its flowers on growth made in the previous year or in the current year. Roses which flower once only produce their flowers on previous year's growth; repeat-flowering roses, necessarily, flower on the current

A floriferous and shapely bush of the Portland 'Comte de Chambord' showing the results of skilful pruning

year's growth. Single-flowering bush roses (which include, for example, Albas, Centifolias, Damasks and Gallicas) should be pruned after flowering to encourage new wood on which flowers will be produced the following year. This should be a light pruning only, to remove weak growth and thin out overcrowding; if you prune too energetically you may promote excessive sappy new growth which will be vulnerable to the first frosts. Repeat-flowering roses (which include, for example, Bourbons, Hybrid Musks, Hybrid Perpetuals, some Moss roses and Portlands) should be pruned in late winter or very early spring. Thin or weak growth should be removed, as should over-crowded stems, especially those rubbing together; and stronger growth may be cut back by a third to encourage vigorous new flowering growth. But in pruning any bush that naturally assumes an attractive shape, do respect the natural habit of growth and avoid over-pruning. Only Hybrid Teas and other modern roses which flower more or less continuously should be pruned heavily (in late winter), with at least two-thirds of the previous year's growth removed. This frequently results in rather absurd-looking plants, with flowers that are too large for their size, but a Hybrid Tea's greatest merit lies in its profusion of flowers, and if left to its own devices it will make a rather scrappy bush.

The pruning of Rambling and Climbing roses follows the same essential principles. Ramblers flower only once on previous year's growth, so should be pruned, if at all, after flowering. Climbers (which includes Noisettes, Hybrid Teas, Climbing Teas and Hybrid Perpetuals which either have climbing sports or are used as climbers) flower more than once on current year's growth, so should be pruned in late winter. Unless they need to be held in check for reasons of space, Ramblers need no pruning apart from the removal of dead wood. Climbers on the other hand do need quite careful pruning. Once a framework of strong growth has been established, lateral growth off the main stems, or any shoots that have flowered the previous year, should be pruned back by about two-thirds in late winter.

Training Climbing Roses

All gardeners will be familiar with the idealised diagrams in gardening books of climbing roses trained into a faultless fan, with no branches overlapping. I have never managed to achieve this; nor, it seems, do even the most expert rose gardeners in some of the very best public rose gardens. But it is a desirable goal, and it is certainly worth trying to achieve as much horizontal or semi-horizontal growth as you can – both to cover the wall and because you will have a greater number of vigorous flowering shoots erupting from horizontal stems.

Climbing roses do need to be properly supported. On a wall, heavy-gauge wires fixed horizontally 12in/30cm apart with regular supports in the form of vine-eyes along its length, every 10ft/3m or so, is an

A climbing rose secured with knotted osiers at La Roseraie de l'Haÿ

immense convenience. When tying in roses to the wires use soft gardening string, never nylon or, worst of all, plastic-covered wire ties which look horrible and can constrict new growth. In old-fashioned French gardens such as La Roseraie de l'Haÿ, the very skilled gardeners still use traditional slips of osier deftly twisted over to secure the rose shoots.

A wall or sturdy fence will provide a protected environment for more tender roses – sheltering them from the wind and trapping the sun. A pergola or arbour does not afford this protection – so if your garden is cold and suffers from winds, plant only the hardier roses in such exposed positions. The colour of a wall or fence will have much influence on the appearance of a rose planted against it. Limestone walls, with yellow or tawny brown in their colouring, make a beautiful background for cream, apricot or yellow roses. Whereas some red brick makes a very ugly background for certain red roses. In Dutch and French formal gardens woodwork is often painted a very dark green, almost black, which provides a sympathetic background to many colours.

Many of the smaller climbing roses, and some of the more lax bush roses, make excellent plants to train on an upright support in a bed. There are all sorts of suitable iron or withy tripods, trellis obelisks, simple

Illustration opposite: 'Iceberg, Climbing' trained on an ancient limestone wall

Roses in the grand
manner – trained to
frame a statue at La
Roseraie de l'Haÿ

posts and other supports on the market. Tying in and
pruning such roses may present a slight problem,
especially in summer when they are surrounded by
other plants, but the roses are shown to wonderful
effect in this way, and are useful in providing structural
emphasis and introducing vertical elements in the
otherwise horizontal plan. In the great French formal
rose gardens, such as La Bagatelle and La Roseraie de
l'Haÿ, roses are trained round trellis arches to frame an
urn or statue. These great gardens have many inspiring
examples from which owners of quite small gardens
may borrow.

Planting with Roses   Roses have the attractive attribute of associating easily
with most other garden plants. But certain plants make
especially happy partners, and I point to these in the
descriptions of individual roses later in the book. Here
I want to talk in more general terms about some of the
most valuable and versatile of the companion plants.

Decorative small plants in front of bush roses will
conceal the one part of them that is rarely ornamental –
the leggy growth at their base. There are many

Meadow sage, *Salvia pratensis*, makes a brilliant partner for roses. Here with the Hybrid Perpetual 'Sidonie'

herbaceous plants and small shrubs, such as the trailing viola (*V. cornuta*), pinks (cultivars of *Dianthus*), the iris-like *Sisyrinchium striatum*, *Heuchera* 'Palace Purple', or the perennial wallflower *Erysimum* 'Bowles Mauve', which will perform this function admirably. The hardy geraniums are indispensable plants and some of the lower-growing kinds are especially good. *Geranium endressii* 'Wargrave Pink' is an excellent deep pink; *G. sanguineum* 'Album' has delicate white flowers and trailing growth; *G.* × *oxonianum* 'Claridge Druce' has warm pink flowers and a very long flowering season. There are many others that make admirable partners for roses.

Annuals also make good foreground plants with roses. *Nigella damascena* (love-in-a-mist), will look superlative at the feet of roses, as will Venus navelwort (*Omphalodes linifolia*), and both will self-seed in warm gardens. The red orach (*Atriplex hortensis* 'Rubra') is handsome, and although I find petunias (*Petunia* × *hybrida* – usually grown as annuals but in fact

White foxgloves are superb companion plants. Here they intermingle with the rose 'Bourbon Queen'

perennials), rather coarse plants which come in some hair-raising colour combinations, there are some useful pinks, reds and excellent rich purples. The tobacco plant *Nicotiana langsdorfii* is especially good with yellow and cream roses.

Plants with slender spires of flowers of sympathetic colour that rise to approximately the same height as rose bushes are particularly valuable, like the herbaceous meadow sage (*Salvia pratensis*), Jacob's Ladder (*Polemonium caeruleum*), the white form of the biennial foxglove (*Digitalis purpurea albiflora*), or some of the perennial foxgloves, especially the pale yellow *Digitalis grandiflora*. Campanulas are exceptionally valuable and both the purple-blue *C. persicifolia* and its white form, *C. p.* 'Album', which self-seed benignly, are wonderful companion plants.

Medium-sized shrubs will also conceal the inelegant legs of roses, as well as providing neighbourly support for the laxer-growing ones, and often give attractive contrast of flower and foliage. The woody sages are

Purple-leafed cotinus, foxgloves and magenta *Geranium psilostemon* make harmonious companions for the pink rose 'Queen Mary'

excellent in this role, either the common sage (*Salvia officinalis*), its purple-leafed cultivar, *S. o.* 'Purpurascens', or *S. lavandulifolia*. Common lavender (*Lavandula angustifolia*) is one of the very best plants with roses, either as an informal hedge or planted with them in the border. Cistus, with their often aromatic leaves, go well with roses, while the silver-grey foliage of artemisias mingle to lovely effect with almost any rose. The little plum-coloured rounded leaves of *Berberis atropurpurea* 'Nana' are very effective with red and purple roses. The silver-grey foliage of artemisias mingle harmoniously with almost any rose; *Artemisia* 'Powis Castle' is a little tender but very beautiful; *A. absinthium* 'East Lambrook' is bigger and forms an airy pale grey background for roses – those with sharp magenta or red looking particularly beautiful.

Some of the larger shrubs are particularly good as background planting for roses. Cultivars of *Cotinus coggygria* with deep plum-coloured foliage, such as

Informal hedges of lavender lead to an arcade of roses in the rose garden at Mottisfont Abbey

C. c. 'Royal Purple', are indispensable as a background to reds and purples, as is the purple-leafed filbert *Corylus maxima* 'Purpurea', with larger leaves. Both can, incidentally, be cut down every year, producing larger leaves, and making them manageable in smaller gardens. The narrow grey leaves of *Elaeagnus* 'Quicksilver' look beautiful as a background to any rose but especially those with pink or purple flowers.

Some of the really big herbaceous plants are particularly recommended. The cardoon (*Cynara cardunculus*) with resplendent silver-grey leaves will provide both a sympathetic background colour and tremendous architectural presence to a border. The purple-leafed fennel *Foeniculum vulgare* 'Purpureum' produces a cloud of very fine bronze foliage which looks lovely with purples and reds. The biennial thistle *Onopordon arabicum* rises to at least 8ft/2.5m and makes a vast silver-grey candelabra of spreading leaves, difficult to cope with but superb among the bigger

Illustration opposite: white foxgloves, white Jacob's Ladder and ferns compose a decorative foreground to 'Constance Spry'

Sharply clipped box hedges make a perfect edging to borders rich in roses

pink-flowered roses. The larger euphorbias, like *E. characias wulfenii* with its decorative glaucous foliage and yellow-green bottle-brush flowerheads, make a distinguished presence that will enhance any rose.

Climbing roses and Ramblers often form spectacular ornaments on their own, needing no associated planting. Nevertheless, other climbing or twining plants, or tender shrubs trained on a wall, make admirable companions and will extend decorative interest over a long season. Wisterias, both *W. floribunda* and *W. sinensis,* flower long before almost all roses but their decorative fronds of pinnate foliage are beautiful with roses. *Buddleja crispa* is one of the best of the summer-flowering shrubs to intermingle successfully with roses. Its pale lilac flowers and grey felty leaves, almost white underneath, may be trained to form a superb background for almost any colour. Tender ceanothus, such as *C.* × *delileanus* 'Gloire de Versailles', with sweetly scented chalk-blue flowers, will also go well.

Honeysuckle, usually the wild woodbine *Lonicera*

Climbing or Rambling
roses are decorative
trained on supports in
large borders. Here
'Rambling Rector' climbs
a trellis-work obelisk

Honeysuckle, usually the wild woodbine *Lonicera periclymenum*, is an essential cottage-garden associate of roses. But there are other kinds, far less invasive, that can be used to provide exactly the colour you require for your roses. The Chinese *L. tragophylla* has beautiful large tawny-yellow flowers; the flowers of *L. periclymenum* 'Serotina' are a cheerful mixture of cream and rich purple, deliciously scented; and *L. × brownii* 'Dropmore Scarlet' produces dazzling bright scarlet flowers from June onwards right through the gardening season. Clematis are wonderful companions for roses. Different kinds will flower from spring to autumn, with varied colour and character, to provide exactly the effect that is needed. I recommend several different varieties in my descriptions of individual roses.

Two ornamental vines are outstandingly decorative. *Vitis coignetiae* produces immense rounded leaves which turn brilliant colours of russet and yellow in the autumn. It is best with the more dramatic, and large-flowered roses. The purple-leafed wine grape, *Vitis vinifera* 'Purpurea', has dusky plum-coloured leaves that are beautiful with red or purple flowers.

Three plants used for hedging show off the qualities of roses particularly well. Yew (*Taxus baccata*) makes a perfect high background hedge to a large border, and roses are seen at their best against its rich dark green. Box, both the common box (*Buxus sempervirens*) and its small-leafed cultivar *B. s.* 'Suffruticosa', provide the most beautiful crisp green edging to borders rich in roses, and the grey foliage and deliciously scented flowers of lavender (*Lavandula angustifolia*) will make a perfect informal hedge. Its grey foliage and deliciously scented purple-blue flowers go beautifully with roses. Both box and lavender will also serve to conceal the unattractive lower limbs of roses.

These are some of the plants that bring out the best in roses. But roses are not fastidious about the company they keep. One of their greatest charms is that *they* will bring out the best in an immense number of other garden plants.

BUSH ROSES

By bush roses I mean all those roses that normally make a bushy shape and show no inclination to climb or to ramp. They vary immensely in size and character – from the very large and wild, such as the magnificent *R. moyesii* which will easily reach 10ft/3m high, to the miniature 'De Meaux', at no more than 24in/60cm. They also vary strikingly in their shape. Some, like many of the Alba roses have an emphatic upright habit, others, like the Rugosa hybrid 'Max Graf' will spread sideways across the ground to form a bush at least four times wider than its height. Their flowers range from the very large single flowers of 'Frühlingsgold', over 4in/10cm across, to the miniature rosettes of 'White Pet', a mere 1 1/2in/4cm across. In colour of flower they provide infinitely varied shades of white, of pink, of red, or of purple. The character of the foliage varies widely. The European wild rose *R. fedtschenkoana* has the palest grey leaves composed of exquisite miniature leaflets. 'Nyveldt's White' has foliage that gleams like polished leather. They vary in thorns, fruit and the colour of their stems. All these qualities make them irreplaceably valuable garden plants. Beautiful in themselves, they also have the virtue of mixing harmoniously with other garden plants, of providing exactly the right colour or emphasis of shape that may be needed for a particular arrangement.

In even the smallest garden there are bush roses that will fit in with your arrangement. For a small bed there are miniature roses that are perfectly in scale in all their details so that the effect may be identical, in a smaller area, to that of a much bigger rose in a large garden. In a little town garden, for example, the smaller roses may be planted in a bed laid out alongside a sitting area so that their scent and the detail of the plant may be appreciated from close up. In a small garden, where perpetual flowering will be especially valued, there are several roses from which to choose.

Rosa 'Abbotswood'

Origin: Britain (Hilling) 1954
Height: 10ft/3m
Z: 3

This is a hybrid between the European native dog rose, *R. canina*, and some unknown garden variety. It has all the vigour and character of the wild rose but produces flowers of exquisite delicacy in May or June. Opening from elegantly pointed buds, they are 2 1/2in/6cm across, a rich pink, semi-double, with overlapping petals and a froth of smaller petals at the centre. They have the same light, sweet and irresistible scent as their wild parent, and produce a profusion of hips. The leaves are small and edged with fine teeth.

This is no rose for a polite border. It will naturally form a considerable thicket, and its well thorned, vigorous new growth will elbow out more restrained plants. Plant it in an orchard, or naturalistically in an informal hedge, through which it will scramble, throwing out flower-fringed branches.

Rosa 'Alain Blanchard'

Origin: France (Vibert) 1839
Height: 4ft/1.2m
Z: 4

This old Gallica is probably a hybrid with the Provence rose, *R.* × *centifolia*. It has very ornamental buds, long and pointed and fringed with pointed sepals. The partly open flower bud shows a striking deep crimson. The flowers when they open in June are a sprightly crimson, very slightly double, 3in/8cm across, with a very marked bush of egg-yolk yellow stamens. The flowers are slightly cupped at first but open flat, with slightly smaller petals towards the centre, and a light but sweet scent. As they age they become speckled with purple-red, which gives a pretty, marbled effect to the petals. The new foliage is pale green with elegantly creased, slightly toothed leaflets.

'Alain Blanchard' forms a vigorous bushy shrub, almost as wide as it is high, with particularly decorative flowers. It flowers only once but the fresh green foliage will continue to give pleasure. It flowers well in the partial shade and it is at its best in the border where its fine crimson colour will make a dazzling contribution to a scheme of reds and purples. It is a colour that also looks superb against silver foliage – I have seen it against a great curtain of the very pale grey-silver sub-shrub *Artemisia absinthium* 'Lambrook Silver'.

Rosa × alba 'Alba Maxima'

Origin: Europe before 15th century
Height: 8ft/2.5m
Z: 4

This magnificent Alba, also known as the 'Jacobite Rose' and the 'White Rose of York', is a superlative garden plant. Its buds have ornamental lacy sepals, between which the colour of the swelling buds is revealed: a lovely creamy pink. The flowers in June are double, 3 1/2in/9cm across, white with a creamy white

centre and a faint suggestion of pink. As they age, the
green eye at the centre is replaced by a bush of stamens,
the colour fades to white, and the form becomes looser.
It is said occasionally to produce semi-double flowers.
The scent is sweet and spicy. The foliage is extremely
decorative – pinnate, glaucous-grey, with deeply veined
and boldly toothed leaflets. It puts out strong, well
thorned new growth.

This healthy, vigorous rose, with its exceptional
flowers and excellent foliage, is one of the very best of
the old shrub roses. Although it flowers only once, it
flowers for a very long season. It has a good upright
habit, and a bush of 'Alba Maxima' on either side of a
substantial entrance, with no other planting, is a
magnificent sight. At the back of a large mixed border,
its foliage will make an excellent background to other
plants, even after the flowering has finished. There is
also a semi-double flowered cultivar, *R. × alba* 'Alba
Semiplena', with exceptionally graceful flowers with
ruffled petals that are a marvellous pure white. In other
ways it is identical to 'Alba Maxima'.

Rosa 'Ardoisée de Lyon'

Origin: France (Damaizin)
1858
Height: 4ft/1.2m
Z: 5

This superlative Hybrid Perpetual starts to flower
rather late in the season and then flowers repeatedly,
deep into the autumn. The buds are fat and round, and
when partly open reveal a striking deep red with ruffled
petals. The flowers, opening in late June, are superbly
double, 3in/8cm across, deep cerise pink. They always
remain slightly cupped, and the petals are strikingly
arranged: crumpled and swirling in the centre but
neatly deployed in concentric circles at the rim, where
the tips curve sharply backwards. Their scent is
exceptional – a lovely deep, vibrant perfume. The
flowers are held well aloft in lavish clusters and the
plant has bold foliage with curved and pleated pale
green leaflets. It forms an upright, vigorous bush.

All in all, this is among the very best of the Hybrid
Perpetuals. It has exceptional flowers, borne repeatedly
throughout the season, with a marvellous scent. It has
all the decorative qualities of a good old shrub rose, and

Illustration opposite:
'Assemblage des Beautés'

it is particularly suited to the smaller garden. It is excellent in a mixed border but also makes an admirable structural plant of modest size. Plant a pair on either side of a gate, or at the opening of a path; the effect will be striking and effective.

Rosa 'Assemblage des Beautés'

Origin: France 1823
Height: 4ft/1.2m
Z: 4

This is one of the very finest of the old Gallica roses. Its buds are exceptionally decorative: round and fat, with elegant pointed tips to the sepals, they show deep blood-red before the flowers open in June. These are double, 3in/8cm across, a wonderful rich deep carmine in colour, and marvellously scented – spicy and rich. They are very well held at the tips of finely thorned stems, and at first are slightly cupped. Then the petals open out, curving backwards, to form dazzling cushions of colour, eventually fading as they age to dusty purple. The leaves are a pale lime green, elegantly curved and creased down the centre.

'Assemblage des Beautés' makes a neat, vigorous little bush. With its beautiful strong colour, graceful flowers and delicious scent, it would be one of the first choices among the old shrub roses for the smaller garden. It will flower well in the partial shade and is excellent in a modest mixed border, with associated plants in proportion to its size: the purple-leafed sage, *Salvia officinalis* 'Purpurascens', makes a good partner. I have also seen it looking very decorative with waves of pinks of different colours planted at its feet, their perfume intermingling with that of the rose.

Rosa 'Baron Girod de l'Ain'

Origin: France
(Reverchon) 1897
Height: 4ft/1.2m
Z: 5

This Hybrid Perpetual has decorative flowers of a most unusual kind. Its fat, rounded buds are at first the deepest red but open in June into cupped, loosely double flowers of the purest crimson, 2 1/2in/6cm across. The edges of the petals are rimmed with white, a most curious and decorative effect that is emphasised by the crimped tips. As the flowers age the outer petals curve backwards while those at the centre remain cupped. These striking flowers are carried in lavish

clusters, held well above the foliage, and are sweetly scented. The leaves are shapely, rounded and toothed.

With its jewel-like flowers, borne repeatedly throughout the season, and its upright habit, this is altogether an excellent rose, forming a neat, vigorous bush. It has an exotic air and is at its best in an arrangement that focuses attention on it. It should not, for example, be grown with other roses alongside it. In a small bed beside a sitting place it will be sufficiently close to hand for its exquisite details to be savoured. Crimson looks especially beautiful against grey foliage, and the common sage, *Salvia officinalis*, or the narrow-leafed lavender, *Lavandula angustifolia*, both make simple but admirable companion plants. It would make a superb centrepiece in a simple mixed border of grey and purple.

Rosa 'Baronne Prévost'

Origin: France (Desprez) 1842
Height: 5ft/1.5m
Z: 5

A distinguished Hybrid Perpetual, 'Baronne Prévost' has bold double rich pink flowers, 3 1/2in/9cm across, which are well scented. The petals are folded, overlapping and with undulating edges, making the form of the flower especially decorative. Even before the flowers appear in June the fat buds are ornamental, showing deep blood-red between the parting sepals. Flowers are carried in bold clusters, held well aloft on tall stems. They have a delicious scent, spicy and sweet.

The pinnate foliage is glaucous green, and leaflets are pleated and toothed. New growth is very thorny.

This vigorous, healthy bush is an excellent old shrub rose for the mixed border where its decorative foliage and upright habit of growth will also make a contribution. It has the valuable quality of repeat flowering and the deep pink of its flowers, with their bold form, will hold their own among even the most swashbuckling plants. I have seen it looking magnificent with the great silver leaves of the cardoon, *Cynarus cardunculus*, and the tall white-flowered spires of *Campanula latiloba* 'Alba'. Later in the season it would look marvellous with the finely cut grey foliage and blue flowers of the distinguished Russian sage, *Perovskia atriplicifolia*. This is a rose of powerful character and its associated planting should always be bold and simple.

Rosa 'Belle Amour'

Origin: France c.1950
Height: 6ft/1.8m
Z: 4

The origins of this rose are obscure. Discovered by the geat gardener Nancy Lindsay in an old convent garden in Normandy, it is uncertain whether it is an Alba or a Damask. Either way, it is an extremely attractive rose. Its buds are fringed with pointed sepals which when they part show blood-red. The half-opened flower bud is a slightly paler red, very tightly scrolled and most ornamental. The fully open flower in June is double,

3in/8cm across, a warm pink fading to silver-pink, with a sweet and spicy scent. The petals in the centre are loosely quartered and those at the edge form a neat circle. As the flower ages it becomes much looser, revealing yellow stamens. It flowers only once but over a fairly long season. The foliage is handsome, the grey-green leaves well rounded and pointed. It has very thorny new growth.

'Belle Amour' makes a loosely growing but upright bush of character, the pink of the flowers looking marvellous against the grey-green foliage. It is an excellent shrub rose for the large mixed border where it will associate beautifully with larger herbaceous plants such as *Campanula lactiflora* whose tall spires of lilac flowers will intermingle with the rose. The large silver-grey-leafed shrub *Elaeagnus* 'Quicksilver' makes an exquisite background to it.

Rosa 'Belle de Crécy'

Origin: France, before 1848
Height: 4ft/1.2m
Z: 4

The flowers of this Gallica change colour in a subtle and attractive way. When they first open, the buds show a very deep red, with tightly scrolled petals framed in pointed sepals. The flowers in June are double, 3in/8cm across, a clear and lively cerise pink but occasionally smudged with red. Although the flower head is neatly shaped, the petals twist at the tips and turn in different directions, giving a sense of liveliness. The stamens form a striking eye at the centre of the flowers which have an excellent rich sweet scent. As the flowers age they become mauve and eventually paler still. It has elegant foliage and the stems are almost without thorns. Flowers are carried in clusters at the tips of stems, raised well above the foliage.

'Belle de Crécy' is one of those precious old roses which, while having several distinguished features, nevertheless fits in easily with other plants. It makes a slightly lax smaller bush, produces very fine flowers of not ostentatious size in a beautiful colour, and has a delicous scent. It may need a little support from adjacent smaller shrubs; lavender is an excellent partner from this point of view, rising just high enough to support it, and the lavender flowers will echo in colour those of the fading rose.

Rosa 'Belle Isis'

Origin: Belgium
(Parmentier) 1848
Height: 4ft/1.2m
Z: 4

The pure pale pink of the flowers of 'Belle Isis' is rarely seen in Gallicas, and the flowers are also exceptionally small. It has strikingly handsome buds: plump, striped with red and pink, and frilled with ornate sepals. The flowers in June are at first neatly contained: flat rosettes 2in/5cm across with a swirl of pale pink petals at the centre, and an outer rim, like a frame, of paler backwards-curving petals. Later the flowers become much looser, and the colour fades to an even paler pink. Their scent is marvellous – rich, sweet and vibrant. The foliage provides a fine background for the flowers; it is lime green with toothed and rounded leaves. The flowers are carried in generous clusters.

'Belle Isis' forms an upright little bush and carries its charming, deliciously scented flowers well above its decorative leaves. The relative smallness of its flowers compared with those of other Gallicas, which sometimes appear a little top-heavy, gives the plant a lightness and delicacy. This is a quality worth emphasising in associated planting. I have seen it looking marvellous with a froth of the airy little annual navelwort *Omphalodes linifolia* about its feet. Or use it with one of the herbaceous artemisias such as *A. ludoviciana latiloba*, with its decorative lobed and pointed leaves.

Rosa 'Blanche Double de Coubert'

Origin: France (Cochet-Cochet) 1892
Height: 5ft/1.5m
Z: 4

This Rugosa hybrid is one of the most precious white-flowered shrub roses. It is an excellent example of an immensely popular and widely seen rose that nevertheless always retains its charm. Long scrolled buds start to open in May, showing at first a creamy white with hints of pink. When fully open, the flower is semi-double, chalk white, with striking stamens, 4in/10cm across, and perfumed with an excellent spicy scent. The petals overlap and are slightly crimped, and the flower has a beguiling irregularity. Flowers will be produced through the whole season. These are much encouraged by regular deadheading but this will lose you the decorative plump orange-red hips. The foliage is marvellous – a deep, rich glistening green – and each leaflet is deeply veined with a leathery surface.

'Blanche Double de Coubert' is an outstanding rose and forms a distinguished upright bush. It is a very versatile rose: use it in the shade where it flowers well and looks marvellous, or in the mixed border where it will fit in with almost any scheme. It is also quite shapely enough to make an admirable free-standing shrub in a position of importance: a pair flanking the entrance to a path, with their gleaming foliage and cool flowers, would look wonderful. A sport of 'Blanche Double de Coubert' with the lovely name of 'Souvenir de Philémon Cochet' has all its charms, but the flowers are much more double and have a creamy pink centre and a green eye.

Rosa 'Bonica'

Origin: France (Meilland) 1981
Height: 36in/90cm
Z: 4

This modern shrub rose is of a new type widely used in plantings in public places where perpetual flowering, ease of cultivation and a low bushy habit to suppress weeds are especially valued. In the vast majority of roses of this kind these qualities take priority over beauty or character of flower. 'Bonica' seems to me a splendid attempt at breeding a rose for a specific purpose – without losing its charm. It has profuse clusters of fat little buds with pointed sepals which open in June into partly opened flowers of very shapely scrolled shape. They are silver pink on the outside, a much warmer flesh-pink within. When they open fully they are semi-double with a light, sweet scent. The petals are slightly frilly, and finely disposed, arranged in concentric circles and becoming smaller towards the centre. The foliage has shapely mid-green leaves.

I have only seen 'Bonica' used as carpet-bedding to suppress weeds and reduce maintenance. However, this very pretty rose has quite enough charm to make an admirable border plant. Its small stature and profusion of flowers throughout the summer especially recommend it for smaller gardens. Plant it with those herbaceous plants of sympathetic colour that go so well with older roses: silver-blue campanulas and eryngiums, mauve geraniums and pale grey *Artemisia ludoviciana latiloba*.

Rosa 'Boule de Neige'

Origin: France (Lacharme) 1867
Height: 5ft/1.5m
Z: 5

White is an uncommon colour for a Bourbon, and this is easily the best. From purple-pink buds, frilled with decorative sepals, the double white flowers open in June. They are 3in/8cm across, a warmer creamy pink towards the centre, exquisitely formed, with the outer petals curving back slightly, and the inner petals gently cupped. Eventually, when the flowers are fully mature, the petals will curl so far as to make the flowers almost spherical. These have a marvellous rich, spicy scent and are borne profusely at the tips of upright stems, rising high above the foliage. The first flush of flowers is followed by scattered later flowerings. Leaves are mid-green, rather bold, rounded and toothed.

With exceptional scent, recurrent flowering, subtly coloured and beautifully shaped flowers, 'Boule de Neige' would be among the first candidates for a medium-sized white-flowered shrub rose. It forms an upright bush and, as the flowers are carried well aloft, makes a powerful vertical emphasis. The creamy pink tint of the flowers will harmonise easily with other colours – with creams, yellows or blues or with pinks and mauves. Use it in a medium-sized border where a pair would give valuable structure. Or grow it in a pot in a town garden where its neat shape and repeat-flowering will make it a valuable ornament on a sunny terrace. It is said to perform well only in rich soil.

Rosa 'Bourbon Queen'

Origin: France (Mauget) 1834
Height: 6ft/1.8m
Z: 5

This marvellous old Bourbon forms a large shrub and has bold flowers to match. The buds are globe-shaped, frilled with pointed sepals which separate to reveal a mottled rosy red. The flowers in June are very double, 4in/10cm across, an exceptionally beautiful rich carmine pink, and sweetly scented. The flower is slightly cupped at first, with the petals beautifully grouped – folding inwards towards the centre but curving back towards the edges. As the flowers age they open out and take on a languid, informal air, and the colour becomes a lovely faded silver-pink. The foliage is particularly striking: large, rounded and toothed leaves with a dark glaucous-green tinge.

The flowers of this Bourbon are full of character and they are borne abundantly on the tips of vigorous fleshy stems. There is an air of exuberance about it. Unlike some other Bourbons it scarcely ever flowers more than once, but its foliage is ornamental. It flowers well in partial shade and in a large border a pair of bushes will add emphatic structure. The purple-pink of its flower colour is versatile; quite rich enough to mix with reds and purples, it is by no means too overpowering to harmonise with a softer scheme of pale pinks and blues.

Rosa 'Buff Beauty'

Origin: Britain (Bentall) 1939
Height: 5ft/1.5m
Z: 5

This Hybrid Musk is deservedly popular and has much more character than many more popular roses. The buds are exotic: plump with pointed sepals which as they part show pink and yellow. The flowers when they are newly opened in early June have a marvellous shape, the centre tightly scrolled and the outer petals curling backwards. At this stage the colour is a warm yellow apricot. When they open fully they become much blowsier and much paler, ivory suffused with pale yellow. The petals curl and bend backwards, making a very full flower, 3 1/2in/9cm across, and with a lovely sweet rich scent. The foliage is striking, with large, shapely dark green leaves, some of which are as long as 4in/10cm. The flowers are carried in generous clusters on upright stems which are handsomely tinged with red-brown.

'Buff Beauty' flowers constantly through the season, and at any moment shows the attractive contrast of opening bud, newly opened flower and fully open flower. However, the striking beauty of its flowers is not matched by the bush itself. Although vigorous, and throwing out gracefully curving new growth, it does not form a shapely bush and it is at its best in a mixed planting. It will make a valuable contribution to a lively scheme of creams, yellows and orange. Try it among daylilies or intermingled with the July-flowering panther lily, *Lilium pardalinum*.

Rosa 'Camaïeux'

Origin: France 1830
Height: 36in/90cm
Z: 4

This old Gallica produces its flowers in June from shapely, plump deep red buds with pointed sepals. The flowers are double, 3in/8cm, pink but striped irregularly with crimson purple, and with a warm spicy scent. As the flowers age they become more loosely blowsy and fade to a grey-purple. The foliage is a fresh mid-green, and new growth is covered in very fine hair-like thorns.

The growth of 'Camaïeux' is rather lax, and as the bush becomes burdened with weighty flowers, branches tend to flop down. This is part of its charm but it will need support, either from other plants in a closely packed border or by some artificial means. It has not the firmness of shape to contribute to the structure of a border but it is at its most decorative towards the front where its lovely flowers will rise above other plants. Plant it among decorative small shrubs such as the sage *Salvia officinalis* 'Tricolor' whose variegated leaves are splashed with pink, and with lavender; both will make excellent companions.

Rosa 'Canary Bird'

Origin: China, c.1908
Height: 8ft/2.4m
Z: 5

A hybrid of two Chinese species, *R. xanthina hugonis*
and an unknown rose, 'Canary Bird' has many virtues.
The foliage is very delicate, unfurling, just before the
first buds open, in elegant fronds, each leaflet minutely
toothed and of a fine grey-green with much paler
undersides. The single flowers, each 1 1/2in/4cm
across, are of a distinctive pale yellow, becoming darker
towards the centre which is filled with dark gold
stamens. The flowers have finely rounded petals but
almost no scent at all. One of the earliest roses to
flower, in favoured places, 'Canary Bird' will produce
its first flowers as early as late April. The new growth
of the stems is a decorative dark bronze and the hips
are also strikingly dark. It is very healthy although the
occasional branch may have a tendency to die back,
when it should be pruned back in the usual way.

'Canary Bird' has all the distinction of a wild rose
but it is by no means too wild for the border, where it
makes an excellent spring-flowering shrub. Later in the

season, even without flowers, the distinctive foliage makes it a good border ornament. Beware, however, of planting other yellow-flowered plants close to it unless they are of the palest colour. Grey-leaved shrubs – artemisias, lavender or santolinas – look excellent at its feet. It is also available grown as a very pretty standard.

Rosa 'Capitaine Basroger'

Origin: France
(Moreau-Robert) 1890
Height: 6ft/1.8m
Z: 5

Moss roses often have such a vivid character in all their details that just one in a small garden can make a tremendous contribution. 'Capitaine Basroger' has the characteristic moss-covered buds which, as they start to open, show pretty stripes of pink and crimson. The flowers in June are fully double, 3in/8cm across, deep crimson in colour, sombre and beautiful. In spite of the flowers' neat shape, curved and folded petals swirl in a lively pattern. They are marbled with veins of a deeper colour and there are flecks of pink in the crimson. As the flowers age the colour becomes pink-purple. The scent is exceptional – deep and rich. The foliage is grey-green with big, rounded leaflets.

'Capitaine Basroger' forms an upright, rather loose bush and, unusually among Moss roses, it produces a second flowering at the end of the season. The flowers are heavy and new growth rather lax, so a certain amount of support will be needed. Its rich colouring makes a telling contribution to a bold scheme of reds and purples, but it is perhaps best of all in a position where its lovely flowers and delicious scent may be appreciated close to. Grow it all alone in a sunny corner, with a path or a seat nearby.

Rosa 'Cécile Brünner'

Origin: France
(Pernet-Duchet) 1881
Height: 36in/90cm
Z: 4

This perpetual-flowering dwarf Polyantha has very pretty flowers and is an extremely ornamental and versatile garden plant. The emerging flower conveys the very essence of an idealised rose bud – it is pale pink, neatly formed, gently scrolled and frilled, with prominent star-shaped sepals. The developing flower passes through two more stages. At first it is gently cupped, exquisitely framed by the backward curving, much paler outer petals. Eventually it ages to a blowsy little pompom, becoming pure white. At its fullest extent the flower is no more than 2 1/2in/6cm across. It is well scented, with a sweet clear perfume, and the flowers are carried well aloft on upright stems, an attractive red-brown in colour. The shapely foliage has elegantly pointed, rather long leaflets.

At the front of a border, or filling some little bed close to a sitting place, or in countless other positions, the lovely flowers and perpetual flowering of 'Cécile Brünner' are of immense value. Although dwarf, it is perfectly proportioned and the individual flowers have all the character of something much bigger. It is an excellent rose for a pot, where it must be well watered and fed. The white form, 'Cécile Brünner, White', identical in all other respects, mixes very successfully with the type. A climbing form, 'Cécile Brünner, Climbing', is slightly less perpetual than the type but is an admirable climber where space is limited.

Rosa 'Céleste'

Origin: Netherlands
18th century
Height: 6ft/1.8m
Z: 4

Also known as 'Celestial', this Alba is an outstanding large shrub. Its buds are particularly beautiful – very long and pointed with whiskery sepals. As they swell, the flower colour shows through, a creamy pink. The flowers in June are semi-double, 3 1/2in/9cm across, a lively shell-pink fading to silver-pink in parts. The subtly veined petals undulate and slightly overlap, and at the centre of each flower smaller petals swirl round the prominent stamens. The flowers are borne in generous clusters at the tips of stems and have a delicious sweet scent with spicy undertones. The foliage is glaucous-grey with boldly toothed and veined leaflets.

The fragile beauty of these flowers is very striking against the grey foliage. This is a substantial shrub – strong and upright – for a large border where it will give bold structure and fit in harmoniously with many other plants. It flowers only once but its handsome foliage makes an excellent background for other plantings. Train one of the smaller, later flowering clematis, such as *C. viticella* 'Etoile Violette' up it; the rich, dark purple will look splendid against the grey.

Rosa 'Celsiana'

Origin: Europe before 1732
Height: 5ft/1.5m
Z: 4

This is one of the earliest surviving cultivars of the Damask rose and one of the most beautiful of pink-flowered roses. The buds, forming in late spring, are very beautiful, framed in an intricate lacework of sepals which part to reveal the red flower bud. The flowers open in June, semi-double 3in/7cm across, a lovely clear shell-pink, slightly cupped at first but opening fully to a slightly blowsy fullness. Their scent is marvellous – spicy and warm. The foliage is pale green with elegant leaflets, creased and finely toothed. The flowers are carried well aloft in clusters, on pale green finely hairy stems.

This is not an ostentatious rose but the more one looks at it the more attractive it appears. It flowers only once – but it flowers memorably. The flowers are beautiful and the whole bush with its good upright habit has an air of distinction. It is superb in the centre of a generous border, especially in the company of grey-leafed shrubs such as santolinas and artemisias, which provide an excellent foil for the pink flowers. The herbaceous clematis, *C. integrifolia rosea*, with flowers of a rather deeper lilac-pink, looks wonderful threading through it.

Rosa × *centifolia* 'Cristata'

Origin: Switzerland
c. 1820
Height: 5ft/1.5m
Z: 5

This Moss rose is also widely known as 'Chapeau de Napoléon', a reference to the very decorative mossy calyx which does indeed resemble Napoleon's tricorn hat. The buds are very mossy and the sepals of fern-like intricacy. The flower buds inside are scarlet, and open in June into beautifully formed double flowers, 3in/8cm across, rich cerise-pink but silver-pink on the backs of the petals. The flowers are marvellous – at first slightly cupped, and when fully open retaining a strong shape with swirling concentric petals with outward-curving tips. The perfume is excellent – deep and warm. The foliage has pale green toothed leaflets, some of which are edged with red. New growth is downy and red-brown in colour.

Both buds and flowers of *R.* × *centifolia* 'Cristata' are decorative. The plant has a rather lax growth and the flowers are big and heavy, so it is best supported, either artificially or by other shrubs in a border. It has a

Illustration opposite:
Rosa 'Charles de Mills'

strong identity and will certainly not be lost in a mixed border. Grow it with smaller grey shrubs, with cistus or with the attractively grey-leafed *Caryopteris* × *clandonensis*, which will help to support it and provide harmonious company.

Rosa 'Cerise Bouquet'

Origin: Germany (Kordes) 1958
Height: 12ft/3.6m
Z: 4

Despite its genteel name 'Cerise Bouquet' is full of character. It forms a substantial (too substantial for smaller gardens) bush with small rounded leaves of an excellent grey-green. The flowers in June, carried in lavish bunches, have something of the character of the old shrub roses – they are double, 3in/8cm across, a rich pink-crimson. They have a light but fruity scent, and a second flush of flowers is often produced later in the season. New growth is made in the form of splendid, arching stems. It will do well in partial shade.

Unlike most modern shrub roses 'Cerise Bouquet' has a wild, vigorous character. The flowers, very profusely borne on the bold new growth, are beautiful against the grey foliage. It is at its best when left to grow unchecked into a large bush, erupting with new growth. It grows quickly, making gnarled woody growth that gives the appearance of antiquity. This is no rose for a polite border – it is best in a very informal setting. Grow it in an orchard, or among trees or other large shrubs.

Rosa 'Charles de Mills'

Origin: Unknown
Height: 4ft/1.2m
Z: 4

No other rose has quite the colouring of this resplendent Gallica. Very plump buds fringed with twisting sepals at first show a flower colour of the deepest blood-red. When the flowers open in June they are very dark crimson-red, double, 4 1/2in/11cm across. At first they are neatly formed but they become blowsier as they age. At that stage the undulating petals are seen to vary in size, and many are frilly at the tips, which gives the flower head a lively, informal appearance. At the centre the flowers are lightly striped and smudged with pink and white. The scent is curious, not like that of any other rose, but smelling vaguely of

sweet wine. The leaves are dark green, boldly toothed, and have a gleaming surface. Flowers are carried in clusters on tall stems rising well above the foliage.

The uncertainty of its origin, and its sumptuous and sombre flowers give 'Charles de Mills' an exotic air; its older name of 'Bizarre Triomphant' is perhaps more expressive of its character. It is very vigorous, flowering only once but carrying its flowers over a long period. It forms a bush almost as wide as it is high. Grow it among reds and purples where it will make a powerful contribution. A pale grey background, perhaps an artemisia, shows off the flower colour beautifully.

Rosa 'Commandant Beaurepaire'

Origin: France
(Moreau-Robert) 1874
Height: 5ft/1.5m
Z: 5

This exotic Bourbon makes a striking ornamental plant. Plump spherical buds at first show deep red between the sepals. They open in June, at first into elegantly cupped flowers, framed in twisting sepals, pale pink but striped and smudged in carmine and purple. When they open fully they are 3in/8cm across, semi-double, with lively undulating and curving petals and a delicious sweet scent. The foliage is exceptionally decorative – lime-green with toothed leaflets.

The flowers of 'Commandant Beaurepaire' are among the most beautiful of the parti-coloured roses and are repeat-flowering. They are very profusely borne and their striking colour will make a powerful contribution to a border colour scheme of pinks, reds and purples. Bold shrubs with plum-coloured leaves, such as *Cotinus coggygria* in one of its purple forms, or *Berberis thunbergii* 'Atropurpurea', make admirable companions. 'Commandant Beaurepaire' forms such a strong, well-leafed shrub, and its foliage is so striking that even when not in flower it has a strongly decorative presence. It will flower well in partial shade and, with plenty of watering and feeding, it makes a superb plant for a pot.

Rosa 'Complicata'

Origin: Europe 20th century
Height: 6ft/1.8m
Z: 4

The origins of this rose are obscure; it is certainly very close to some wild parentage and is possibly a cross between the two European natives, *R. gallica* and the dog rose, *R. canina*. From these it inherits its wild vigour, while its flowers resemble those of *R. gallica* but are much more graceful. They open in June from shapely pointed buds and are single, 3in/8cm across, a warm pink fading to a much paler centre with profuse

Illustration opposite:
Rosa 'Comte de
Chambord'

egg-yolk yellow stamens. The flowers are slightly cupped at first, with overlapping petals of very fragile appearance, but when they open fully the petals spread and twist, giving the flower a lovely character. The star shapes of the sepals and the striking bush of stamens are ornamental, and hips form while the plant is still in flower.

Some roses make an immediate impact but while 'Complicata' is scarcely shy and retiring, its full beauty and character reveal themselves gradually. It will naturally form a rather floppy bush, with slender new growth arching down to the ground. Use it in a large border, where other shrubs will provide support for 10ft/3m stems which will then make a spectacular display. Or train it into the lower branches of a tree where its beautiful flowers will be given prominence.

Rosa 'Comte de Chambord'

Origin: France
(Moreau-Robert) 1860
Height: 4ft/1.2m
Z: 4

This Portland rose is a hybrid between the beautiful Hybrid Perpetual 'Baronne Prévost' (see page 44) and *R*. 'Portlandica'. Its identity is a little uncertain and its correct name may be 'Madame Knorr'. Although not typical of the group, it is one of the most beautiful. The buds have pointed, rather hairy sepals, and open in June to double flowers, 3 1/2in/9cm across, a lovely rich pink at the centre, fading to pale shell-pink at the edges. The petals have frilly tips, are curved and folded, and arranged loosely in quarters, giving the flowers a lively texture and splendid fullness. They are deliciously scented, with a sweet vibrant perfume. The foliage is a good grey-green with shapely leaves, and the flowers are held in generous clusters well above it on stems bristling with fine red thorns. After the first profuse June flowering it will flower continuously throughout the season.

'Comte de Chambord' makes a vigorous free-flowering bush and is among the very finest of old roses, especially for smaller gardens where its compact size and perpetual flowering will be particularly appreciated. Although it is full of character it is extremely versatile. Use it as a hardworking ingredient

in a mixed border, or for some structural purpose. Because of its very long flowering season, it will accompany sympathetic June-flowering plants like campanulas and geraniums, and at the end of the season will also make a brilliant partner for late summer shrubs such as *Caryopteris × clandonensis*. It is a rose that should be on every gardener's short-list.

Rosa 'Conrad Ferdinand Meyer'

Origin: Germany (Müller) 1899
Height: 8ft/2.5m
Z: 4

This hybrid of *R. rugosa* and *R.* 'Gloire de Dijon' makes a substantial bush with beautiful, deliciously scented flowers in June. These, 3in/8cm across and double, are at first cupped but open fully into flowers of languid beauty which, after the first flush, will continue throughout the season. Deadheading will encourage this but it does mean that you will be deprived of the very decorative hips. The scent is exceptionally good – deep and sweet and wafted great distances on a breeze. The healthy foliage is veined and slightly leathery, a good dark colour.

This large healthy bush, with its distinguished flowers and scent, can be used to make a substantial structural contribution to a border. It has a tendency to become top-heavy and it should be pruned heavily. 'Conrad Ferdinand Meyer' is quite vigorous enough to make a useful climber if trained on a wall or up a post.

Rosa 'Cornelia'

Origin: Britain (Pemberton) 1925
Height: 5ft/1.5m
Z: 5

'Cornelia', a sweetly scented recurrent-flowering Hybrid Musk with handsome foliage, makes an exceptionally decorative garden plant. The buds, carried on plum-coloured new growth, are a curious

colour: a rich pink, flecked and suffused with yellow. As they open, with crowded and crimped petals, they resemble pinks. The flowers in June are loosely double, 3in/8cm when fully open, a striking mixture of warm pink and silver pink. The petals are slightly cupped, undulating and overlapping attractively. The colour fades to a much paler pink as the flowers age. They have a light sweet scent. Flowers produced later in the season are said to be a deeper colour. The foliage is dark green with boldly shaped leaves.

With its lavish clusters of flowers, good scent, striking foliage and vigorous habit 'Cornelia' is a thoroughly garden-worthy plant. It forms a spreading bush, at least as wide as it is high, and may be used successfully as an informal hedge. Try it also trained against a low trellis or balustrading, over which it will flop decoratively, flowering generously throughout the season. In a mixed planting in the border its lively colouring will harmonise well with reds and purples. Among herbaceous perennials its solid form will give structure.

Rosa 'Coupe d'Hébé'

Origin: France (Laffay)
1840
Height: 6ft/1.8m
Z: 5

This delightful, stately Bourbon rose is well named – it has all the freshness and sparkle of the goddess of spring and youth. The double flowers in June, 2 1/2in/6cm across, resemble handfuls of crushed silk, a marvellous rich pink with purple overtones, cupped and never opening fully. The tips of the outer petals curve back sharply, and the inner petals remain scrolled. The flowers are borne abundantly in groups at the tips of tall stems and have a rich, spicy scent. The new shoots are vigorous and thorny and the leaves are pale green, shapely and boldly toothed, making an admirable foil to the flowers. It is prone to mildew.

Many of the Bourbons are irresistible but the great beauty of 'Coupe d'Hébé' lies in the liveliness of its flower colour and the generous profusion of its blossoming. It makes a substantial bush, and flowers repeatedly through the season. Use it as the focal point of a big border but beware of planting it near other pinks which may suffer in comparison and appear insipid. It looks wonderful with lavish waves of rich violet *Viola cornuta* lapping at its feet, or with the tall spires of the larger campanulas, such as blue or white *Campanula latiloba* interweaving through its branches. The giant thistle, *Onopordon arabicum*, with the palest grey leaves, makes a spectacular companion.

Rosa × *damascena semperflorens*

Origin: Ancient garden rose
Height: 5ft/1.5m
Z: 4

This was formerly known under the name of 'Quatre Saisons'. It is the original 'Autumn Damask', one of the oldest of all repeat-flowering rose cultivars, and it is from this rose that Damasks derive their ability to repeat-flower. It is strikingly ornamental before coming into flower: a profusion of beautiful pointed buds, bristling with the twisting tips of the sepals, are carried on pale green shoots with fine red thorns. In June the flowers open, generous, double, pale pink, 3in/8cm across, perfumed with a deep rich scent. The petals curl and twist giving the flowers a lively and informal character, and the golden eye of the stamens is half hidden by a ring of smaller petals at the centre. The pale green leaves, boldly rounded and toothed, make an excellent foil to the flowers. There is also a white form,

'Quatre Saisons Blanche Mousseuse', identical in all other respects.

R. × *damascena semperflorens* forms an upright vigorous bush and, being ornamental, recurrent-flowering and deliciously scented, makes an excellent plant for some prominent and accessible position. A pair flanking the opening of a path, or on either side of a door, is very effective. The silver pink of the flowers ensures that it will fit in either with a richly coloured scheme of reds and purples, or with a much cooler arrangement of creams or soft mauves (such as lavender or the paler forms of *Viola cornuta*).

Rosa 'De Meaux'

Origin: Britain (Sweet)
before 1789
Height: 24in/60cm
Z: 5

This little Centifolia, also known as 'Rose de Meaux', among the smallest of the old varieties to survive, is a most decorative miniature rose – but it has all the character of something much larger, scaled down in perfect proportion. The buds are very ornamental, frilled with lacy sepals. They open in June into perfectly formed rosettes, 1 1/2in/4cm across, tightly furled and slightly cupped at first, but opening flatter. They are a lively pink, turning a paler silver-pink towards the edges and are only slightly scented. The petals are folded and slightly frilled at the tips, giving rather the appearance of a carnation. They are borne profusely and carried at the tips of stems well above the foliage. The leaves have rather the character of a wild rose: grey-green, rounded and slightly toothed. There is also a white form, *R.* 'De Meaux White', which looks very pretty mixed with the pink form.

Delicacy is the most striking quality of 'De Meaux'. It looks wonderful in the company of pinks, which are only a little shorter and produce remarkably similar flowers. It is tempting to plant it at the front of a full-scale border but it is at its best in a miniature setting. In a very small garden an accurately scaled-down border could be made with 'De Meaux' as its *pièce de résistance*, underplanted with diascias, the smallest geraniums (such as *G. sanguineum striatum*) and violas. Although it flowers only once, its foliage will continue to give pleasure through the season.

Rosa 'De Rescht'

Origin: Iran late 1940s
Height: 36in/90cm
Z: 4

This is also known as 'Rose de Rescht' and its origins are vague; all that can be said with certainty is that it was introduced into English gardens after World War II by Miss Nancy Lindsay who probably acquired it in Iran. It is a wonderfully ornamental Damask of rare and exotic beauty. From tight spherical buds the flowers open in June. They are double, 2 1/2in/6cm across, a beautiful crimson in colour, with a golden eye of stamens almost concealed at the centre. The petals swirl in lively patterns and the tips of some curl over revealing a paler underside. The flowers are at first very neatly shaped but become looser with age. Their scent is among the very best – deep, rich and marvellously exotic. The leaves are grey-green, rounded, pointed and finely toothed. New growth is very pale green and covered in fine red hair-like thorns. Young bushes will produce more flowers intermittently after the first flowering; it is said that, as the bush gets older, its remontancy will be encouraged by hard pruning.

So often the most glamorous roses prove too large for smaller gardens. 'De Rescht' is one of the most ornamental of smaller shrub roses. It forms a neat bush and the flowers are carried in generous clusters on rather short flowering stems – so they appear to be cushioned on a bed of foliage. It could be used in many different circumstances: in a mixed bed, in a pot, flanking a path or doorway. At all events, make sure that it is close enough to a path or terrace for its wonderful scent and beautiful flowers to be appreciated.

Rosa 'Dembrowski'

Origin: France (Vibert)
1849
Height: 4ft/1.2m
Z: 5

This richly coloured Hybrid Perpetual should be seen more frequently in gardens. Its buds show rich red as the sepals part, and the new open flower in June is exquisitely formed, neatly scrolled and framed in gracefully curving outer petals. The colour is a vibrant cerise-pink and the petals are etched with a deeper colour. The fully open flower is 3 1/2in/9cm across, still slightly cupped, with petals arranged in loose quarters about a green eye at the centre. As the flower ages it becomes a lovely warm silver-pink. The foliage is beautiful, with rather languid pale green pointed leaflets, and new growth flushed with bronze.

'Dembrowski' is an outstanding rose for the smaller garden. It does not grow too big, is perpetual flowering, and the progression of colours, from deep

red buds to faded silver flowers, is extremely ornamental. It is rather lax in growth and needs support, but can be used as an admirable climber, flowering well in partial shade. It could be the dominant plant in a small mixed border with a harmonising colour scheme. The tall swaying flowers of the perpetual-flowering *Knautia macedonica*, a deep purple-red, look magnificent with it. As an underplanting, *Geranium endressii* 'Wargrave Pink' would be very pretty – with pale pink flowers and decorative leaves.

Rosa 'Du Maître d'Ecole'

Origin: France (Meillez) 1840
Height: 36in/90cm
Z: 4

This sumptuously flowered Gallica is the ideal old shrub rose for the smaller garden, expressing the whole character of the type on a small scale. Its buds show blood-red between the splitting, pointed sepals, but the magnificent double flowers in June, 3in/8cm across, are a rich deep pink with deeper tones of magenta at the centre and silver-pink at the edges – like some delicious dessert of crushed berries and cream. The flowers are

tightly cupped at first but when they open out the petals are beautifully displayed – folded and ruffed, arranged in swirling quarters. The flowers eventually open fully, revealing a curious green eye at the centre, and finally fade to a distinguished lilac. They are richly perfumed. The pale green foliage has neat little pleated leaflets, and new growth is covered in down.

This will make a sturdy little bush with the marvellous flowers swaying outwards, weighing down their branches. Use it as the key shrub in a small border, determining the whole colour scheme: it associates best with purples, plums or rich reds. Plant it with the shrub *Abelia grandiflora* with bronze new foliage (and much later on, scented pink trumpet-shaped flowers), the herbaceous *Potentilla atrosanguinea* with trailing stems bearing deep blood-red flowers, or *Heuchera* 'Palace Purple' with its plum-coloured foliage.

Rosa 'Duchesse de Buccleugh'

Origin: France (Robert) 1860
Height: 6ft/1.8m
Z: 4

This is one of the most splendid of the Gallicas, with flowers of a rich magenta-pink. The developing buds are very decorative; at first they are neat little plump pale green globes fringed with pointed sepals which part to reveal a striking blood-red within. The partly open flower is long and scrolled, a beautiful faded purple-pink, opening in June to a dazzling and lively

purple-pink, fully double, 3in/8cm across. The petals are arranged in rough quarters in the centre but in overlapping concentric rings at the edge. The foliage has pale green toothed leaflets with strikingly marked veins, and the flowers, which are very sweetly scented, are carried in clusters on long stems that bristle with very fine thorns.

There are so many truly mediocre roses to be found in gardens, yet one rarely sees 'Duchesse de Buccleugh', which is a rose of wonderful character, ornamental in every way. It forms a vigorous, quite bushy shrub which, in the grandest of mixed borders, will still make its presence felt. 'Duchesse de Buccleugh' is among the larger Gallicas and, although it flowers once only, it is a spectacular sight when in flower. The sprightly magenta of its flowers would enliven a rich but sombre scheme of reds and purples; it would also fit in with an arrangement dominated by pinks and blues. In either case its striking foliage, imposing size and emphatic structure will make a powerful contribution.

Rosa 'Duchesse de Montebello'

Origin: France (Laffay)
1829
Height: 4ft/1.2m
Z: 4

All the details of this old Gallica contribute to its air of distinction. Its buds are plump, almost spherical, with lacy sepals that project beyond their tips, giving the appearance of a miniature artichoke. After the sepals have parted, the flower bud shows a lovely creamy colour smudged with pink. The buds are carried in clusters at the tips of stems, borne well aloft, and the flowers in June are double, 3in/8cm across, a pale creamy pink with a green-yellow eye, and with a light sweet scent. The petals have a silky fragile appearance, and some of them curl upwards at the tip, giving the flower a graceful shape. The dark green foliage has toothed leaflets, elegantly creased down the middle, and, in new growth, edged with red. The bush has an upright bushy habit.

There is an appropriately feminine character to the 'Duchesse de Montebello', and although the flowers are marvellously ornamental this is not an ostentatious rose. It will adorn any border, but one should be careful not to overpower it with innappropriate planting. Plants with flowers of cream or pink will look best: cultivars of *Monarda didyma*, such as the pale pink 'Beauty of Cobham', for example, the pink-mauve-flowered *Thalictrum aquilegiifolium*, and creamy white *Sidalcea candida*.

Rosa 'Duchesse de Verneuil'

Origin: France (Portemer)
1856
Height: 5ft/1.5m
Z: 5

This is one of the best of the pink-flowered Moss roses.
The buds are exceptionally ornamental, covered in
moss and with intricate pointed sepals. When the bud
first opens it is a rich red; it then forms a very elegant
little scrolled rich pink flower. When the flower opens
fully in June it is double, 3in/8cm across, with loosely
packed swirling petals, an excellent lively pink, with a
very good sweet musky scent. It has distinguished
foliage with slender, pale green, toothed leaflets, and it
forms an upright bush with the flowers well displayed
against the foliage.

'Duchesse de Verneuil' flowers only once but it is a
splendid flowering, with a profusion of bold flowers of
distinction. It is at its best in a mixed planting,
associating with plants that have complementary
colours. Its handsome pale-coloured foliage will

Illustration below: *Rosa
eglanteria* hybrid 'Amy
Robsart'

continue to be ornamental when the bush is not in
flower. It looks beautiful against the tender *Buddleja
crispa* with pale lilac flowers and felty leaves that are
almost white. The tall catmint *Nepeta* 'Souvenir
d'André Chaudron' makes an excellent foreground
plant, screening the non-flowering parts of the rose and
providing tall spires of clear blue flowers.

Rosa eglanteria

Origin: Europe
Height: 8ft/2.5m
Z: 4

Formerly known as *R. rubiginosa*, the sweet briar is a
lovely wild rose with a graceful habit, decorative
foliage, pretty flowers and, a rare quality in a rose, the
most deliciously scented leaves smelling, especially
after rain, of apples. Some fastidious gardeners would
regard it as too wild for the garden; I grew it among
apple trees in an orchard where it never failed to give
pleasure. However, there are some lovely cultivars and
hybrids, with more glamorous flowers, that are
certainly garden-worthy. The wild type has hairy
flower buds with tufted sepals which open in June to
deep pink, 1in/2.5cm across, paling towards the centre

and with bold stamens, and sweetly scented. The foliage is an attractive grey-green with elegant little finely toothed leaflets. The hips in late summer are bright red, still preserving the tufted sepals seen on the flower bud. The hybrid 'Amy Robsart' has much bigger flowers than its parent, 3in/8cm across, semi-double, a beautiful silvery magenta with heart-shaped petals. The foliage resembles that of its parent but is dark green. 'Greenmantle' has single flowers, 3in/8cm across, a striking carmine with paler centres and prominent stamens. Its foliage is a handsome glaucous-grey.

R. eglanteria forms a tall, lax bush with very prickly growth and is certainly not a rose for the formal border. It should be grown in the wilder parts of the garden, and in an informal hedgerow will scramble upwards, festooning the surrounding growth with its flowers. Although the sweet briars flower only once, they are decorative from the moment their leaves appear in the spring until the last hips are eaten by birds in the winter. They are, in any case, worth having for the fortissimo scent of apples alone, and if they are clipped to encourage a tidier shape, it is from the foliage of the new growth that the strongest scent of apples comes.

Rosa 'Fantin-Latour'

Origin: France c.1900
Height: 6ft/1.8m
Z: 5

The flowers of this modern shrub with the character of an old Centifolia are among the most irresistible of any rose. Striking red buds, with long pointed sepals rising beyond the tip, open in June into double flowers, 3 1/2in/9cm across, a pale and lovely pink occasionally blotched with deeper colour. A swirling mass of petals is tight packed, and clusters of flowers are produced in lavish profusion. The scent is exceptionally good – rich, deep and sweet. The foliage is very striking; bold mid-green leaves have a shining, slightly leathery surface and marked veins.

Although it flowers only once, its flowering is so marvellous as to make it one of the best bush roses. 'Fantin-Latour' is wonderful in a border where its

upright shape and flowers that harmonise easily with other plantings are at their most valuable. The flower colour is delicate and it associates most beautifully with pale silvery blues. Some of the sea-hollies, such as *Eryngium bourgatii* or *Eryngium alpinum*, look marvellous planted in quantity at its feet. Taller herbaceous perennials of sympathetic colouring, such as the lilac-coloured meadow sage *Salvia pratensis* and the pale violet forms of *Campanula latifolia* ('Gloaming' is a good one), go extremely well with it.

Rosa fedtschenkoana

Origin: Central Asia
Height: 8ft/2.5m
Z: 4

I find this elegant wild rose irresistible and I hope I can persuade you of its charms. It has neat little buds with pointed sepals from which emerge in June pure white single flowers, 2in/5cm across, with a prominent bush of lemon-yellow stamens. The petals have a fragile, silky appearance and undulate attractively at the tips. Hips covered with ruddy bristles and crowned by star-shaped sepals start to form very shortly after the first flowers appear. *R. fedtschenkoana* will flower intermittently through the season, by the end of which there is a delightful mixture of orange-red hips and snow-white flowers. The foliage is very beautiful: pale glaucous grey with shapely, strikingly toothed leaflets gently folded down the middle. New shoots are

covered with fine red thorns. It will form a bold upright bush.

The foliage of this lovely rose is so beautiful, and the recurrent flowers scarcely less so, that it will go effortlessly with almost any colour scheme in the mixed border, holding its own with the most sophisticated plants. Its marvellous foliage will make a fine background for almost any planting. *R. fedtschenkoana* will, however, be equally at home in a wild garden set among trees.

Rosa 'Felicia'

Origin: Britain
(Pemberton) 1928
Height: 4ft/1.2m
Z: 5

This is one of the best of the Hybrid Musks, forming a neat bush with beautiful flowers. The buds look slightly misshapen, but show a rosy pink between the opening sepals. The flowers, however, as they open in June are exquisitely formed, with rolled shell-pink petals in the middle, and paler silver-pink petals curling backwards on the outside. When the flowers open fully they are double, 3in/8cm across, blowsy in a refined

sort of way, pale pink with slightly frilly tips to the petals. They have a clear sweet scent and the foliage is a healthy fresh green.

Lightness and refinement define the character of 'Felicia'. The irresistibly ornamental flowers, produced in quantity, the good scent and neat habit make it an excellent garden plant. In smaller gardens it can impart the excitement of something much larger, and since it is recurrent-flowering, it may be used in a dominant position. In a modest mixed border it will associate beautifully with white and blue-mauve plants, and smaller shrubs such as cistus, lavender and sage all make harmonious companions. I have seen it used to lovely effect planted with mauve and white forms of the stately trumpet-flowered *Campanula latifolia* which grows to about the same height and matches the rose for sprightly beauty.

Rosa 'Félicité Parmentier'

Origin: France early 19th century
Height: 4ft/1.2m
Z: 4

This is one of the smaller Alba varieties – and one of the best. Its buds are enclosed in hairy ornamental sepals which part to reveal a fat faded-yellow bud. Buds are held high in lavish clusters. The flowers in June are 3in/8cm across, double, shell-pink at the

centre but much paler towards the edge. They are are slightly cupped at first, with packed petals at the centre and outer petals curving backwards. The fully opened flower forms a beautiful flat rosette, with a striking green eye in the middle. As the flowers age they fade to a glorious creamy pink. They are well scented – light but sweet – and the grey-green foliage has striking toothed leaflets.

'Félicité Parmentier' is not only smaller than other Albas, it is also more compact, forming a very neat bush. Use it as a key plant in a modest mixed border in a small garden, where it will give the full Alba experience. Although flowering only once, it has a long flowering season, and its habit and fine foliage extend its ornamental interest. Its colouring harmonises well with the range from white to red but it also looks beautiful with mauves such as that of the catmint *Nepeta* 'Souvenir d'André Chaudron'. As with other Alba roses, perfectionist gardeners are recommended to thin clusters of buds to two or three in order to produce much bigger flowers.

Rosa 'Ferdinand Pichard'

Origin: France (Verdier) 1869
Height: 5ft/1.5m
Z: 5

'Ferdinand Pichard' is a 20th-century Hybrid Perpetual that has all the character of something much older. Its buds are fringed with pointed sepals which part to reveal a lively rosy red. In June the triumphant flowers are revealed; double, 3 1/2in/9cm across, white but striped and splashed with crimson. The centres of the flowers remain slightly cupped but the outer petals curve backwards, displaying their stripes which radiate outwards from the centre. The flowers, which are carried on tall stems held above the foliage, have a sweet scent. The foliage is handsome: mid green shapely leaves with toothed edges and a glistening surface.

This is one of the finest of the roses with parti-coloured flowers. It is particularly healthy and forms a bush of substance, almost as wide as it is tall. It flowers perpetually throughout the season. Grow it as the decorative centrepiece of a border dominated by pinks and pale blues. In a very small garden it would make an excellent choice if you have room for one rose only. On a terrace in the town, planted in a large pot, it would make a superb ornament. To flower well it must have a sunny position, and it should be deadheaded meticulously.

Rosa 'Fimbriata'

Origin: France (Morlet) 1891
Height: 5ft/1.5m
Z: 4

A Rugosa hybrid with memorably beautiful flowers. They open in June from elegant pointed buds with sepals that project far beyond the tip. The opening flowers are at first strikingly like pinks (indeed it used to be called 'Dianthiflora'). They are shell-pink in the centre, fading to a very pale pink at the rim, but as they open out fully into loosely double flowers, 2 1/2in/6cm across, they become the palest pink all over. The tips of the petals are frilly, which gives the flower a lively character. The flowers have a curious scent, rather like soap, and the foliage is a gleaming light green.

Delicacy and decorativeness are the essential qualities of this exceptionally attractive rose. It flourishes in light shade where the flowers will retain

Illustration opposite:
Rosa 'Ferdinand Pichard'

their soft colouring for a longer time. Both the flowers, which continue to appear throughout the season, and the decorative foliage give the plant an air of distinction. It will grow into a dense upright bush, making it perfect for a structural position in a border, or flanking the opening to a path.

Rosa foetida 'Persiana'

Origin: Britain (Willock) 1837
Height: 5ft/1.2m
Z: 4

It seems almost perverse to include in this book a rose which not only lacks a good scent but has a positively unpleasant one – some authorities report that it smells of bedbugs. But the smell is not strong; to experience it you would have to take a close sniff. The reason for recommending the rose are the very beautiful flowers in high summer, of a colour not exactly matched by any other rose in that season. They open in June from decorative plump buds, at first cupped and globular but at the height of their development opening out almost flat, double, 3in/8cm across. Curling, overlapping petals give a lively appearance, and at the centre smaller petals intermingle with the stamens. The colour is a rich warm golden-yellow – without a trace of that rather acidulous synthetic yellow found in too many modern roses. The foliage has grey-green, finely toothed little leaflets with a shining surface. To flower well it must have a sunny, protected position.

In habit it makes an upright, thorny, distinctly wild-looking bush. It will give character to a mixed border where its splendid rich yellow flowers and grey foliage will make a marvellous contribution to a colour scheme of blue, cream and yellow.

Rosa × francofurtana

Origin: Europe, garden, before 1583
Height: 4ft/1.2m
Z: 6

The identity of this rose is mysterious. It is widely known as 'Empress Josephine' (or 'Impératrice Joséphine') and was grown in her great collection at La Malmaison. But it is much older than that, an ancient garden hybrid, and was described in a Frankfurt garden in the 16th century. It is usually classed as a Gallica but its parentage is very vague. This fine rose has decorative, well-rounded buds crowned with a little tuft of sepals. When they open in June the new flower is delicately cupped, a warm carmine-pink colour, but the fully open flower is double, 3 1/2in/9cm across, rich cerise-pink at the centre and silver-pink at the edges, with gracefully crimped and undulating petals. It has a good spicy scent. The foliage is mid-green, with striking deeply veined and creased leaflets.

The dramatic flowers of *R. × francofurtana* are well set off by the handsome foliage. It is a rose of strong character and will hold its own – and make a decorative contribution – in a mixed border. The flower colour, on the purple side of pink, goes well with a flamboyant red and purple colour scheme. Here, the cool grey of artemisias or cardoons makes a marvellous contrast.

Rosa 'Frau Karl Druschki'

Origin: Germany
(Lambert) 1901
Height: 6ft/1.8m
Z: 5

White roses in full sunshine can sometimes be almost painfully dazzling. The flowers of the Hybrid Perpetual 'Frau Karl Druschki' have depths of cream which make them much more sympathetic. The first flowers appear in June – generous, double, cupped, 3 1/2in/9cm across and carried in groups. The buds are purple-pink and a hint of pink remains in the fully opened flowers, which have a faint but sweet scent. The leaves are attractive, boldly shaped, slightly toothed and a fine glaucous-green. The new growth is fleshy with many thorns. Like other large-flowered white roses it is susceptible to rain damage but is generally a very healthy rose.

Perpetual-flowering white roses with flowers of

distinction are particularly valuable garden plants. 'Frau Karl Druschki', with its aristocratic bearing, used to be among the most popular of roses. Use it a mixed border, with rosy-pink cistus and soft blue campanulas, set off with grey foliage; it will make a striking contribution. Or use it as a most valuable element in a white or generally pale-coloured border. A climbing form, with a height of up to 15ft/4.5m, has all the virtues of its more earthbound sister.

Rosa 'Fritz Nobis'

Origin: Germany (Kordes) 1940
Height: 5ft/1.5m
Z: 5

There is some Hybrid Tea character in the very mixed parentage of this modern shrub rose, but it has none of the coarseness and lack of proportion that marks too many Hybrid Teas. 'Fritz Nobis' produces an immense number of buds which have much of the charm of the old shrub roses: they are plump, with long pointed sepals at first and open gradually to show a splendid rosy pink. Fully open in June, the flowers are double, 3in/8cm across, an excellent warm pink, with a good spicy scent. The petals are slightly crimped at the edge, loosely quartered, and curve backwards towards the edge of the flower where they become much paler. 'Fritz Nobis' flowers only once but produces a tremendous display of flowers over a long period. The leaves are handsome: bold, rounded and toothed, some strikingly large, up to 3 1/2in/9cm long. It produces huge quantities of orange hips in the autumn.

This has all the vigour and health of many of the modern roses but its flowers belong to an older tradition. It will form a big bush, almost as wide as it is high, and in full abundant flower it will look magnificent in a large mixed border where its handsome foliage will also be an ornament. It is so vigorous that it can also very successfully be trained as an excellent climber; here its flowers will be even better displayed than as a bush. Use it in this way in smaller gardens where the bush might seem out of scale.

Rosa 'Fru Dagmar Hastrup'

Origin: Germany
(Hastrup) 1914
Height: 5ft/1.5m
Z: 4

There is an irresistible sparkling freshness, in flower and foliage, to this Rugosa hybrid. The buds are characteristically Rugosa – decorated with tapering pointed sepals and forming a long, scrolled shape showing a deeper shade of the flower colour just before opening. The flowers in early June are single, 4in/10cm across, a glistening silver-pink with a bold tuft of golden yellow stamens and a sweet scent. The petals have a silken fragile quality, and twist, giving the flowers a languid, informal character. Flowers are produced repeatedly throughout the season. The foliage is outstandingly good: deeply veined, rather leathery leaves are pleated down the centre, and have a gleaming polished surface. The hips are marvellous – a dazzling crimson – and they take on their colour fairly early, appearing at the same time as the flowers.

In many ways this is an ideal border plant. It will flower well in partial shade where its sparkling foliage will be seen at its best, and it flowers throughout the season. It has strikingly decorative foliage and hips, and forms a shapely bush. Its flower colour will harmonise with many other plants, and can be used effectively in the smaller garden as the most important plant in a mixed border.

Rosa 'Frühlingsanfang'

Origin: Germany (Kordes) 1950
Height: 8ft/2.5m
Z: 4

One of the great achievements of modern rose breeders has been to introduce varieties that make the best of the wild character of the parent roses with which they work. This one, a cross between the Scotch rose, *R. pimpinellifolia*, and a garden rose, is a splendid example. Its shapely buds open in June into magnificent ivory-white single flowers, 4in/10cm across. When the flower is at its peak the heart-shaped petals, whose tips are slightly crimped, separate entirely, giving the flower a most striking appearance. The petals have the texture of thin silk and their shape is emphasised by the pattern of veins that sweep outwards from the tuft of twisting stamens at the centre. The scent is curious, more like a peony than a rose. The fine foliage, with its delicate toothed leaflets, show the plant's Scotch rose parentage. It has splendid hips, and the foliage colours well in the autumn.

This is a splendid aristocrat of a rose, with wild distinction in all its parts. It will form a strong thorny bush and it would be a mistake to coop it up in a border or in any formal setting. I have seen it in a small arboretum in partial shade, looking marvellous with other large roses and substantial shrubs like *Viburnum plicatum* and *Hydrangea quercifolia*.

Rosa 'Frühlingsgold'

Origin: Germany (Kordes) 1937
Height: 7ft/2m
Z: 4

Kordes's great shrub roses with their wild character are among the most distinctive, and precious, modern garden plants. The elegant long scrolled buds of 'Frühlingsgold' show their primrose-yellow colour quite early in May, and the flowers open before the end of the month. Certainly among the most spectacular of the early flowering roses, they are very big, fully 4 1/2in/11cm across, semi-double, slightly cupped, pale primrose and deliciously scented with a sweet perfume. The tuft of golden stamens looks especially striking against the deeper yellow of the centre of the flower. As they age the flowers fade to a warm ivory which makes a lovely contrast to the yellow buds. The neat foliage shows its *R. pimpinellifolia* parentage, with elegantly toothed, slightly grey leaflets.

'Frühlingsgold' forms a large open bush with splendid arching stems on which the flowers are profusely carried. It is an exceptionally healthy, trouble-free rose which will flourish in almost any soil and flower well in partial shade. It is a wonderful plant for a substantial spring border where it will come into flower as the last flowers of *Magnolia stellata* fade. It looks magnificent soaring over tall clumps of the yellow-flowered *Euphorbia characias wulfenii*. It will be perfectly at home, too, in a wilder garden setting.

Rosa gallica var. officinalis

Origin: Near East
Height: 4ft/1.2m
Z: 4

The Apothecaries' Rose, also known as the Rose de Provins, was possibly brought to Europe during the crusades in the 13th century, and was certainly known by the year 1400. Its medicinal properties were recognised by Arab physicians, and it was later harvested in quantity for that purpose in Europe. (The *officina* in a monastery was the store-room where medicines were kept.) It has very beautiful plump blood-red buds, fringed with pointed sepals, which open into big, semi-double flowers, 4 1/2in/11cm across, with exquisite fragile petals the texture of fine silk. At first a sumptuous magenta-red, the colour fades to a carmine-pink and the flower shape changes from slightly cupped to fully open, revealing a bold bush of stamens. The scent is marvellous – a vibrant warm spicy perfume. The plant has pale green foliage with rather leathery, emphatically veined leaflets. The hips in autumn are a striking brick-red and rather hairy.

Brilliant colour, particularly graceful form of flower, and exceptional scent are the distinctive qualities of the Apothecaries' Rose. I have seen it used as a splendid informal ornamental hedge in a kitchen garden, making reference to its ancient practical use. It will also make a sprightly contribution in a mixed border with a red and purple colour scheme.

Rosa gallica 'Versicolor'

Origin: Europe, Asia
before 1583
Height: 36in/90cm
Z: 4

Also known as 'Rosa Mundi', this cultivar of the wild rose, *R. gallica*, is one of the most ancient garden roses and one of the oldest cultivars of any plant. But it is not merely its historic interest that earns its place in the garden today, for it is an exceptionally decorative rose. Shapely buds, a beautiful flame red, in generous clusters, open in June to reveal semi-double flowers of attractively floppy form, 3 1/2in/9cm across, pink but handsomely striped and spotted in crimson, and deliciously scented – warm and spicy. The petals overlap and undulate, giving the flower a lively appearance. Although quite a small rose, new shoots are rather lax and tend to collapse to the ground with the weight of flowers, so they may need support. The foliage is a fresh pale green with deeply veined long and pointed leaflets, and new growth is covered in very fine thorns.

'Rosa Mundi', because of its suckering habit, makes an admirably decorative and exotic hedge which may be shaped loosely after flowering. I have seen it flanking a narrow stone path, making a lovely scented walk. Its exotically striped flowers are carried in great abundance over a long period, and against simple paving or bricks it has a triumphantly decorative character.

Rosa 'Gertrude Jekyll'

Origin: Britain (Austin) 1987
Height: 4ft/1.2m
Z: 5

This modern shrub rose has many of the best qualities of the old roses, combined with the vigour and perpetual flowering of the modern varieties. The buds are very decorative, rounded with twisting points of sepals, and showing, as they start to open, a striking crimson-red. The flowers in June are fully double, 4 1/2in/11cm across, cerise-pink, shading to a paler pink at the edges. The petals are packed in, swirling in different directions but arranged in a loosely quartered pattern. They are exceptionally well scented, with a warm spicy perfume. Flowers are borne in lavish clusters, held well above the foliage which has leaves that are boldly rounded and toothed, of a shining deep green. New foliage and shoots are tinted with bronze.

'Gertrude Jekyll' is particularly to be recommended for the smaller garden where its abundant, constant flowering and bold character in a compact form will be particularly valuable. Use it to form the chief shrubby ingredient of a modest border, setting the theme for a lively colour scheme of reds and purples; or in a larger scheme, where it has quite enough presence to make a telling contribution. I have seen a pair planted in very large pots on a terrace; they looked superb, and their delicious scent perfumed the air.

Rosa 'Glamis Castle'

Origin: Britain (Austin)
1992
Height: 36in/90cm
Z: 5

David Austin regards this new rose as the best white he has bred so far. Plump buds tinged with pink open very early, even in April, into sumptuous double white flowers 4in/10cm across. They are slightly cupped, with the petals on the edge curving backwards and those towards the centre curving inwards, giving the flower a charming shape. The flower colour is not pure white and towards the centre it is a pale creamy pink. It has a faint musky scent. The foliage is bold and a little coarse. It will flower continuously right through to the autumn.

It is the beautiful flower alone that earns this rose a place in the garden. There are countless ways in which its decorative qualities could be used but it will always be at its best in association with other planting. Because it flowers so perpetually and prolifically, and because the white is so subtly modulated, it would be equally successful in a chiefly white scheme or one in which cream, pale pink and soft blues are used. On a terrace, or in a small garden, plant it in a pot to make a marvellous ornament.

Rosa glauca

Origin: Central and
Southern Europe
Height: 8ft/2.4m
Z: 2

This was previously known as *R. rubrifolia*. There are few roses which are decorative throughout the gardening season; *R. glauca* is an exceptional example. Its leaves are especially beautiful – a lovely grey suffused with red – delicate, slightly toothed, edged in red and creased down the middle. The flowers in June emerge from dusty red buds with pointed tips and are single, a sharp pink becoming paler, with a white centre and prominent stamens, 1 1/2in/4cm across. In late summer and autumn the hips are a glistening scarlet and well shaped. It is very healthy and one of the very hardiest of roses. It will seed itself gently – seedlings should be chosen for the beauty of the foliage which shows subtle variations.

The habit of growth – upright and with tall arching stems – makes this an admirable rose for the mixed border where it will give structure and where its lovely foliage will rise above other plantings. The leaf-colour goes well in almost any setting but is at its very best in a hot colour scheme of reds and purples. The rich purple flowers of *Gladiolus communis* look marvellous with it, and the smaller dark purple-flowered *Clematis viticella* may be trained up its stems to excellent effect.

Rosa 'Gloire de France'

Origin: France before 1819
Height: 36in/90cm
Z: 4

This old Gallica, with its sumptuous flowers and sweet scent, is one of the best of the roses with double rich-pink flowers. The buds are almost globular but pointed at the top and well framed by pointed sepals. These unfurl in June, opening out into exceptional double flowers, 3in/8cm across, a rich cerise-pink at the centre but fading to silver-pink at the edges. The centre petals, lavishly packed in, are folded and have curved tips, while the outer petals curve back sharply until, as the flower ages, it becomes almost globe-shaped. By this time the colour has faded to an off-white suffused with lilac. The flowers have a good sweet scent and are borne profusely, carried well above the foliage on tall hairy stems. The foliage is a handsome pale green.

This profusely flowering small shrub has flowers that are generous in form and quantity, lovely in colour, and sweet in scent. Like other Gallicas it is inclined to be lax in growth but it makes a rather spreading bush, as wide as it is tall, which means that it is less top heavy than others. It is, in any case, at its best among other plants, which will help to support it. Lavenders and sages look very well – especially *Salvia officinalis* 'Tricolor' whose leaves are prettily splashed with pink.

Rosa 'Golden Wings'

Origin: USA (Shepherd) 1956
Height: 5ft/1.5m
Z: 4

This modern hybrid, one of whose parents is the Scotch rose, *R. pimpinellifolia*, is one of the very best of all yellow-flowered shrub roses, retaining much of the character of its wild parentage. Its buds, just before the flowers open, are wonderfully decorative – long and flagon-shaped, fringed with pointed sepals, a lovely lemon-yellow. The flowers open in June, single but with double tendencies, a warm primrose-yellow, 3 1/2in/9cm across, with a sweet scent. The petals curve and some are frilled, giving an impression of movement, and the centre is ornamented with very striking golden-brown stamens. The foliage has grey-green slightly toothed leaflets. It forms a healthy-looking vigorous bush with open growth and branching stems with few thorns.

'Golden Wings' flowers profusely and perpetually throughout the season and is best in a sunny position. Although it has much of the bold wild character of much larger roses, such as the 'Frühlings' series, its compact form makes it suitable for smaller gardens. It is a wonderful rose in a mixed border with a pale colour scheme, looking beautiful, for example, with the creamy yellow flowers of the perennial foxglove *Digitalis grandiflora* and the sharper yellow of *Verbascum bombyciferum*.

Rosa 'Great Maiden's Blush'

Origin: Europe 15th century
Height: 6ft/1.8m
Z: 4

This great Alba, one of the oldest surviving garden varieties of rose, is also one of the finest of all garden plants. The buds are lovely – creamy pink, plump, slightly hairy and encased in airy, pointed sepals that extend far beyond the tip of the bud. The flowers in June are double, pale pink, 3in/8cm across, with an excellent spicy sweet scent. The flowers are at first slightly cupped and very neatly formed but as they age they become abandoned and fade almost to white. Many flowers are carried on each stem. The foliage, characteristic of the Alba group, is wonderfully decorative – glaucous-grey with well-rounded toothed leaflets. In France it is known as 'Cuisse de Nymphe' ('nymph's thigh') and there is a beautifully named deeper pink clone, 'Cuisse de Nymphe Emue'.

Although flowering only once, 'Great Maiden's Blush' flowers over a very long period and, with its fine foliage, makes a distinguished bush that is ornamental throughout the season. Its bold upright form has tremendous presence – one at each end of a large border would have a powerful unifying effect. Its subtle colouring, in both flower and foliage, and its discreet beauty, make the choice of companion planting difficult. Avoid anything coarse or raucous but do not be half-hearted; other bold plants of different character, such as the great cardoon *Cynara cardunculus* or the silver-leafed shrub *Elaeagnus* 'Quicksilver', make excellent partners.

Rosa 'Gros Choux de Hollande'

Origin: Unknown
Height: 6ft/1.8m
Z: 5

The identity of this Bourbon rose is shrouded in mystery, and it seems that the name is sometimes misapplied to other roses. The particular specimen I have seen and admired is in the garden at Kiftsgate Court (which has a famous, and marvellous, collection of old roses). Very attractive rosy-pink buds open in June into lavish double flowers, 4 1/2in/11cm across, a beautiful rich pink. The crowded petals curve either backwards or forwards at the tip, and swirl in different directions. The tips of some of the petals are frilly and a paler colour than the centre. Although the flowers are held well up above the foliage, the stems are slender and the weight of the heads tends to make them flop forwards. They have a sweet spicy scent. The foliage is mid-green with rounded, boldly toothed and pointed leaves. The fleshy new growth is very pale green with very fine thorns.

'Gros Choux de Hollande' makes a substantial and vigorous bush. Its lavish and unusually large flowers are in proportion and it is magnificent in a large mixed border. Grow it with pale blue campanulas and geraniums, choice cultivars of taller growing geraniums like *G. pratense*, or *Campanula latifolia* whose spires associate splendidly with it.

Rosa 'Gruss an Aachen'

Origin: Germany (Geduldig) 1909
Height: 24in/60cm
Z: 5

Many of the very best 20th-century roses were bred in the early years of the century and have gone out of fashion for no very good reason. 'Gruss an Aachen', a continuous-flowering Polyantha with delightful flowers and a good scent, is an excellent garden plant. Its rosy red buds, framed in pointed sepals, open in June into double creamy pink flowers, 3 1/2in/9cm across, and sweetly scented. They are held handsomely aloft and are very neatly shaped with a profusion of folded fragile-looking petals. As the flowers age they lose their pink and become cream. The dark green foliage is not particularly distinguished.

This would be one of the very best roses to use in some prominent place in the smaller garden. It flowers throughout the season, and the sweetly scented flowers associate well with many other plants. It forms a neat, upright bush and will make a decisive, hardworking contribution to a small-scale mixed border. It looks beautiful accompanied by smaller herbaceous plants in pinks and white, such as diascias and pinks, or with low-growing shrubs with more sprightly colouring, such as *Cistus × pulverulentus*. It is an excellent plant for pots, either by itself, where its neat shape and well-held flowers will be particularly appreciated, or in combination with other plants.

Rosa 'Heather Muir'

Origin: Britain
(Sunningdale Nurseries)
1957
Height: 8ft/2.5m
Z: 6

This great rose appeared as a seedling of the Himalayan species *R. sericea*. From small round buds the flowers open in May. They are single, 2in/5cm across, white, with the palest yellow centre and prominent golden stamens. Their scent is light and sweet. The petals overlap and are slightly crimped at the edges, gossamer thin and etched with ghostly grey veins. Although it flowers only once the season is a long one, lasting at least two months. The foliage is exquisitely attractive: fern-like and composed of many very small finely toothed leaflets. The new growth is strikingly armed with bold red thorns. There are beautiful hips in the late summer: orange-red and elegantly pear-shaped.

It is a marvellous experience to see this wild and wonderful rose in full flower early in the season. Yet its very nature makes it difficult to place in the garden, its artless beauty tending to show up the contrived charms of the more overbred garden plants. 'Heather Muir' forms a substantial thicket, almost as wide as it is high. Grow it in the more naturalistic parts of the garden where it will look wonderful. It flowers well in semi-shade, so a woodland glade with trees and large shrubs would be an ideal setting.

Rosa 'Hebe's Lip'

Origin: Britain (Paul)
1912
Height: 4ft/1.2m
Z: 4

This charming rose is a hybrid between the Damask rose and the European native sweet briar, *R. eglanteria*. Although introduced into commerce in 1912 it is almost certainly very much older. The flower buds are prettily coloured in pink and white and open in June into semi-double flowers, 3in/8cm across. These are white but some of the petals have tips splashed with red, as though dipped in ink. The silky petals curl and undulate, making an animated frame for the very striking egg-yolk-yellow stamens at the centre. They have a light sweet scent. The foliage has much of the character of sweet briar – elegant fresh green leaves, pleated and finely toothed, with the delicious sharp-sweet scent of apples. The new growth, too, shows its wild parentage: it bristles with red thorns.

The special attraction of this rose lies in the contrast between its natural simplicity and the sophistication of its flowers. It makes a striking little bush with twiggy thorned stems – the ideal rose for a busy cottage-garden border in which it will harmonise easily with many other plantings but give a distinctive note of its own. It is not a rose for artful associations.

Rosa 'Henri Fouquier'

Origin: France early 19th century
Height: 4ft/1.2m
Z: 4

As a group the Gallicas, with their beautiful flowers on compact bushes, are among the most precious shrub roses for smaller gardens. The shapely rosy red buds of 'Henri Fouquier', frilled with ornamental sepals, open in June into bold double flowers, 4in/10cm across, with a marvellous deep sweet scent. The colour is a sprightly cerise-pink turning paler on the outer petals. The form of the flower is flat, with a green eye at the centre, and the curved and crimped petals make a lively pattern, loosely quartered. The foliage is an attractive pale green. Flowers are carried in profuse clusters at the tips of stems which are virtually thornless.

'Henri Fouquier' is a precious rose for the smaller garden but it has a rather floppy growth and will need support. Although it has all the glamour of the old shrub roses its rather informal flower shape means that it fits equally well in quite a grand border or with a simple cottage-garden scheme. With *Alchemilla mollis*, *Astrantia major*, lavender and sage it makes a charming, unpretentious arrangement. Silver-grey and blue are also colours that associate well – *Artemisia* 'Powis Castle', *Campanula persicifolia* and *Geranium* 'Johnson's Blue' make an equally satisfying harmony in a different key.

Rosa 'Henri Martin'

Origin: France (Laffay) 1863
Height: 6ft/1.8m
Z: 5

This old Moss rose, also known as 'Red Moss', is one of the most glamorous of its kind. Its buds are well covered in the characteristic spiny 'moss' which splits to reveal the flowers, a very lively crimson. The flowers, which open fully in June, are double, large, 3 1/2in/9cm across, with silky overlapping and undulating petals and a golden eye of stamens glimpsed at the centre. As the flowers develop the outer petals curve backwards and the colour takes on a faded lilac-purple hue. They are carried high on stems bristling with fine hair-like thorns and have an excellent musky scent. The leaves are boldly rounded, slightly toothed, and a good dark green with a gleaming surface.

'Henri Martin' is an emphatic rose in all its details – striking buds, a profusion of flowers, dazzling in both form and colour, shapely foliage and a handsome upright habit. In a big border it would add richness and structural presence to a colour scheme of red and purple. A pair flanking the start of a path or a gate would make a triumphant entrance. At all events, it is not a plant for the timid gardener or the retiring corner.

Rosa 'Hermosa'

Origin: France
(Marchesau) 1840
Height: 3ft/90cm
Z: 5

This old China rose, also known as 'Mélanie Lemaire' and 'Madame Neumann', is an exceptionally valuable garden plant. From plump buds double flowers open in June. They are a lovely shell pink, cupped, 2in/5cm across, with a light sweet scent. They hang decoratively, swaying easily in the breeze, the outer petals attractively curved backwards. The elegant little grey-green leaves are finely toothed.

'Hermosa' forms a healthy, vigorous little bush and flowers repeatedly throughout the season. It is distinguished in all its details. Its great virtue, especially in smaller gardens, is its modest size, and its harmonious proportions avoid the artificiality of some of the modern miniature roses. Use it in a small-scale border, or tucked away in a sunny corner by a terrace, where it will make a most ornamental plant. In company with other plants it is best to keep every thing in scale – the smaller irises, violas, pinks and the smaller geraniums associate well. It is excellent in a pot, either by itself or in the company of other plants. There is also a climbing form, not so free-flowering as the bush, but nonetheless one of the prettiest climbers for restricted space.

Rosa 'Honorine de Brabant'

Origin: Nertherlands before 1850
Height: 6ft/1.8m
Z: 5

I like roses striped or splashed with a second colour. To me they have a festive air, like flags waved in some Renaissance carnival. This Bourbon with the lovely name is one of the best. Its buds are beautiful: as the long pointed sepals separate, the colour within shows pale green and red. The flowers, opening in June, are double, 3in/8cm across, very pale pink, striped and splashed with a deeper pink-purple. When first open they are elegantly cupped, with the tips of the petals curving backwards. Their marvellous scent, sweet and rich, is among the best perfumes of any rose. They are carried in lavish clusters at the tips of pale green new growth that bristles with hair-like thorns. The leaves are bold and shapely, with finely toothed undulating edges.

'Honorine de Brabant' makes a substantial upright bush which will flower well in partial shade. It is perpetual-flowering and will make a major contribution to a big mixed border, but its exotic flowers demand a simple accompaniment. Plant it with the bold lilac spires of field sage, *Salvia pratensis*, or with a background of a large grey-leafed shrub such as *Elaeagnus* 'Quicksilver'. I have seen it looking wonderful emerging from a clump of purple-leafed sage (*Salvia officinalis* 'Purpurascens') and with pale silvery lilac *Geranium pratense* 'Mrs Kendall Clarke'. Plant it also near a path so that its fabulous scent may be fully savoured.

Rosa 'Iceberg'

Origin: Germany (Kordes) 1958
Height: 4ft/1.2m 62
Z: 5

This Floribunda, also known as 'Schneewittchen' and 'Fée des Neiges', is one of the most widely seen modern roses – for very good reason. It produces a profusion of fine flowers and is a very healthy, vigorous rose. It is not, it would be fair to say, a plant of tremendous character, but as a long-lasting ingredient in a planting scheme it has great value. Its pointed buds open at first into beautiful long scrolled buds, creamy white in colour. When the flowers first open in June they are slightly cupped, double, with a cream centre. The fully open flowers, 4in/10cm across, are much looser in shape and still retain some cream to temper the pure white. They are carried in lavish clusters at the tips of stems that rise above the foliage. In many books one reads that the flowers are pure white and have no scent. Neither is true. In addition to their delicately cream colour they have a good scent, light but sweet. In very hot weather the flowers may be curiously freckled with pink. The foliage is a shining dark-green with shapely leaflets. There is also an excellent vigorous climbing form, 'Iceberg, Climbing' which will rise to a

Illustration opposite:
Rosa 'Iceberg'

height of about 15ft/4.5m.

'Iceberg', with its perpetual flowering habit and its handsome flowers, is a precious garden plant. It will flower well in the shade and I have seen it very well used in a subtle scheme of greens and whites, underplanted with hostas and with the speckled leaves of *Pulmonaria rubra*. It will make a good contribution to a mixed border of pale colours. It is perfect for smaller gardens, where perpetual flowering is especially welcome. Use it especially in town gardens, which are often particularly shaded, where it performs beautifully.

Rosa 'Ispahan'

Origin: before 1832
Height: 5ft/1.5m
Z: 4

This old Damask, also known under the romantic name of 'Pompon des Princes', has marvellous flowers produced over an exceptionally long season. Plump blood-red buds frilled with intricate sepals open in early June into sugar-pink half-open flowers, the outer petals curving backwards and those in the centre scrolled into a beautifully neat shape. The fully open flower is fully double, 4in/10cm across, with packed petals arranged in a quartered pattern, deep and lively pink at the centre, paler towards the edges. They have a light but sweet scent. The new foliage is lime-green and the leaflets are elegantly creased. New growth is covered in fine hair-like thorns.

'Ispahan' has among the largest, and most glamorous, flowers of any old rose. It flowers only

once but it starts very early and finishes very late – it is often in flower as late as August. It is a bold and characterful rose and will give its best in bold and exciting company. Use it with some of the really large herbaceous plants – it looks marvellous with the dramatic but delicate spires of *Veronicastrum virginicum* (especially in its pale blue form), the giant silver-leafed cardoon, *Cynara cardunculus*, or tall delphiniums, especially those with lilac or mauve flowers.

Rosa × *jacksonii* 'Max Graf'

Origin: USA (Bowditch) 1919
Height: 24in/60cm
Z: 4

This is a hybrid between *R. rugosa* and the sprawling *R. wichuraiana*; it was formerly known simply as 'Max Graf'. It has the characteristic long Rugosa buds which open in June into single 3in/8cm flowers of a lively carmine colour, lightly scented. The petals have a decorative network of veins in a deeper colour, overlap slightly, and have a white centre and bold stamens. The foliage is wonderfully attractive: long slender pointed and toothed leaflets are an excellent dark green with a glittering surface. It has tawny shoots covered in fine thorns. Its habit is strikingly horizontal: like its *R. wichuraiana* parent it throws out trailing new growth and it will make a shrub at least four times wider than its height.

R. × *jacksonii* 'Max Graf' flowers only once but has a very long flowering season. The flowers look exceptionally distinguished against the beautiful shining foliage which flutters and shimmers in the slightest breeze, and it is this foliage and the unusually sprawling habit that makes 'Max Graf' stand out from other shrub roses. It makes very ornamental ground-cover, and in a border its trailing branches can be used to intermingle decoratively with neighbouring plantings. It does well in part shade and makes good underplanting for a shrub or tree. On a slope, or at the top of a terrace, it will make a cascade of glittering foliage.

Rosa 'James Mitchell'

Origin: France (Verdier) 1861
Height: 5ft/1.5m
Z: 5

This is an especially decorative Moss rose. Its characteristic mossy buds have unusually ornamental intricate sepals which twist about the deep red of the opening bud. The flowers in late June or July are double, a vibrant pink, 3in/8cm across. They are loosely shaped, with petals swerving upwards, and at the centre smaller, twisting petals encircling a tuft of rich yellow stamens. The petals are gently folded down the middle, giving the flowers a lively appearance. The perfume is sweet and fragrant. Eventually the flowers become blowsy, giving a romantic air of lavish abandonment. The foliage has pale-green toothed leaflets, and the vigorous new growth is strikingly flushed with red.

This is a healthy medium-sized shrub with very striking flowers. It is an excellent ingredient in the mixed border, and although it flowers only once, its flowering is rather late in the season and it will contiue for several weeks – well after other single-flowering shrub roses have ceased. Its colour, firmly on the rich side of pink, is versatile. It will look well with blues and mauves but is quite strong enough to hold its own in bolder arrangements of red and purple.

Rosa 'Jeanne de Montfort'

Origin: France (Robert)
1850
Height: 7ft/2m
Z: 5

This stately Moss rose bears sumptuous flowers in scale with its size. Beautiful plump red buds, framed in ornate twisting pointed sepals, open in June into heavy very double flowers, 3in/8cm across, of a lively pink that becomes more silver-pink with age. The petals at the centre swirl about a lavish tuft of stamens and those at the edge curl sharply backwards. The flowers are carried in clusters at the tips of stems. They have a sweet scent, not powerful but distinct. The new shoots are bronze-coloured and covered with very fine hair-like thorns. It will sometimes carry a second flush of flowers in late summer or autumn.

'Jeanne de Montfort' is unusually large for a Moss rose and, with its handsome recurrent flowers, makes a distinguished shrub. It is what in the 19th century was called a 'pillar rose'; its long flexible new shoots can easily be trained up a column. It is still grown in exactly this way in France and can be very effective. Try growing it up one of the columns of a pergola, or trained up a post or trellis obelisk as the centrepiece of a substantial border, emerging from a profusion of the blues and mauves that accompany it so well.

Rosa 'Kathryn Morley'

Origin: Britain (Austin) 1990
Height: 30in/75cm
Z: 5

This English Rose is one of the best pink varieties that David Austin has bred. It starts to flower in June, but produces flowers throughout the season. Fat mottled buds open to very double pale pink flowers, 4in/10cm across, fading as they age to the palest of pinks. The form of the flowers is very beautiful; at first they are slightly cupped, with outer petals curving back to frame the petals in the centre, which are slightly frilly at the tips, curved, overlapping and loosely packed – a marvellous sight. The flowers are carried on tall stems in clusters so profuse that the flowers press against each other. They have an excellent sweet and slightly spicy scent. The foliage is very bold, with rounded and toothed leaves, some of which are as much as 3 1/2in/9cm long. It will perform best in a sunny position.

Grow this rose for the beauty of its flowers and its more or less continuous flowering. It forms a rather squat bush and I think is best used in a densely planted border where it will come into its own among lower-growing shrubs. Its delicate colour will accompany a very wide range of other plants. Plant it with cistus, lavender and sage, or sympathetic herbaceous perennials such as blue or white *Campanula persicifolia*.

Rosa 'Königin von Dänemark'

Origin: Germany
(Flottbeck) 1826
Height: 5ft/1.5m
Z: 4

This, also known as *R.* 'Queen of Denmark', is a stately Alba, exceptionally distinguished in flower and foliage. The buds have pointed curving sepals and the flowers, emerging in June, are double, carmine-pink, 2 1/2in/6cm across, with a sweet scent. The newly opened flower is very neatly formed with densely packed petals arranged in quarters around a green eye. As it ages the flowers become looser with the outer petals curving backwards. The foliage is handsome, glaucous-green with shapely finely toothed and pointed leaves. The new growth has striking red thorns. It forms an upright bush with the clusters of flowers held high.

The combination of the glaucous leaves and lively pink flowers on a substantial bush gives 'Königin von Dänemark' great character. It is an excellent shrub for a place of importance in a mixed border. It flowers only once, for a long season, but the foliage and shapely habit will give valuable structure to a border. The combination of pink and blue-grey is always decorative and may be carried over very effectively into other associated plantings. The much paler grey of artemisias, *Elaeagnus* 'Quicksilver' and santolina, and the blues of campanulas and eryngiums such as *E. bourgatii* look marvellous with this rose.

Rosa 'La Belle Distinguée'

Origin: Garden before 1790
Height: 4ft/1.2m
Z: 4

Also known as 'Scarlet Sweetbriar' and 'La Petite Duchesse', this very unusual old rose is thought to be a hybrid between the European native sweet briar, *R. eglanteria*, and some unknown garden rose. It has beautiful delicate foliage with very finely toothed grey-green leaflets. The foliage has the distinctive sweet briar scent of apples. Striking plump red buds open in June to reveal flat double flowers, 2 1/2in/6cm across, a bright pink with a touch of carmine, fading to silver-pink in parts. The petals are folded, with scalloped edges, which give the flowers an animated appearance.

Forming an erect dense little bush, with a great profusion of flowers, 'La Belle Distinguée' is perfectly in scale, which makes it an excellent ingredient in a scaled-down border. Its cheerful colour gives it great presence in a colour scheme of red and purple with touches of cool grey. Plant it with the narrow-leafed sage, *Salvia lavandulifolia*, the dark plum-coloured leaves of *Heuchera micrantha* 'Palace Purple' and the deep red flowers of *Potentilla atropurpurea*. In larger borders it looks beautiful in the front, fringed with pinks whose flowers echo in shape those of the rose.

Rosa 'La Noblesse'

Origin: France 1856
Height: 5ft/1.5m
Z: 5

This splendid shrub rose is rarely seen – and yet it is one of the loveliest and most worthwhile of the larger Centifolias. The buds are splendid: plump and beautifully formed with a tuft of pointed sepals which, as they open, show a lovely deep red. The flowers open in June and are fully double, 3 1/2in/9cm across, rich pink in the centre but fading to silver-pink at the edges. They have a sweet musky scent. When the flowers first open the petals are beautifully arranged: those in the middle swirl hither and yon in a roughly quartered pattern; those on the outside are neatly arranged in an enclosing ring, with the outer petals curving sharply backwards to form a circular frame. Flowers are carried in lavish clusters held well aloft at the tips of finely-thorned stems. The grey-green foliage is very handsome with bold leaves.

'La Noblesse', as its name suggests, has stately presence. It forms a shapely bush, and in full bloom, with its magnificent flowers well set off against its foliage, is indeed a noble sight. It could dominate a mixed border where it will look lovely with softer or richer pinks and with mauves such as that of the billowing spires of the meadow sage, *Salvia pratensis*. It flowers only once but its long flowering season takes it well into the peak period of herbaceous plants.

Rosa 'La Ville de Bruxelles'

Origin: France (Vibert) 1849
Height: 5ft/1.5m
Z: 4

This is a magnificent old Damask with sumptuous flowers. Its buds are especially beautiful, ornamented with lacy pointed sepals which part to show rich blood-red. The flowers in June are very double, 3in/8cm across, warm silver-pink, with a sweet light scent. In the centre the petals are arranged in quarters framed by concentric rings of petals that curve backwards and are a much paler pink. The flowers are carried in bold clusters held high above the foliage on pale green new growth speckled with fine red thorns. It will produce occasional scatterings of flowers after the main summer flowering. The foliage is especially handsome, with pale green leaflets, toothed and strikingly veined, up to 4in/10cm long. They are fine in texture, rather floppy, and flutter in the breeze.

'La Ville de Bruxelles' is very much a rose for the mixed border. It forms a vigorous upright plant but since new growth is rather lax it will need supporting either artificially or by other shrubs closely planted. Its exceptionally fine flowers look marvellous among the partly opened deep red buds and their warm pink will make a precious contribution to different colour schemes. Plant it with either blues and pale pinks, or in a more exciting scheme of reds and purples. It looks especially good with some of the larger herbaceous perennials such as *Campanula latiloba* with its spires of purple-blue flowers.

Rosa 'Le Havre'

Origin: France (Eudes) 1871
Height: 4ft/1.2m
Z: 5

This is one of the smaller Hybrid Perpetuals, with splendid flowers and good scent. Some idea of its vigour is given by the fat blood-red buds which seem to be bursting out of their sepals. The flowers, which open in June, are double, 3in/8cm across, deep cerise with purple undertones and a warm spicy scent. The outer petals curl over backwards at the tips, giving the flower a graceful form. The petals in the centre,

surrounding a green eye, are more muddled. After the
first flowering it will flower repeatedly throughout the
season, but will need to be deadheaded regularly. The
foliage is strikingly handsome, with large pale green
leaves, rounded and toothed, with a gleaming slightly
leathery surface.

'Le Havre' is one of those precious repeat-
flowering roses, ornamental in every way and with
dashing old rose character, that is ideal for smaller
gardens. Although of modest size it is full of vigour and
makes a shapely bush. It will flower quite heavily late
in the season, at the same time as some of the most
desirable late-flowering shrubs: it looks wonderful with
the Russian sage, *Perovskia atriplicifolia*, with its
aromatic finely cut grey leaves and spires of
lavender-blue flowers, or with the smaller-growing
Caryopteris × *clandonensis* with blue flowers and
decorative foliage.

Rosa 'Leda'

Origin: Britain before
1838
Height: 36in/90cm
Z: 4

This delightful little rose is also known as 'Painted
Damask', which gives a better idea of its appearance. It
has characteristically Damask buds, very prettily frilled
with ornate sepals. The buds at first show a deep
blood-red but the flowers that open in June are pale
cream with a hint of pink, occasionally splashed with
crimson at the tips of the petals. They are fully double,
2in/5cm across, and sweetly scented. The centre of the
flowers, where the colour becomes strikingly creamy
pink, is marked by a rosette of smaller inward-curving
petals. The flowers are held high in clusters at the tips
of stems bristling with very fine red-brown thorns. The
foliage is very distinguished – large rounded grey-green
leaves with boldly marked veins.

With its jewel-like flowers carried well aloft above
the striking foliage, 'Leda' is one of the best of the
Damasks. It makes a neat bush and is an excellent
ingredient in a mixed border of modest size. Its
colouring makes it very versatile, harmonising easily
with a wide range of other flowers. Plant it with some
of the larger pinks, such as the white 'Mrs Sinkins',

spreading about its feet. Lavender-blue also goes well with the cream and crimson: the tall, swaying double flowers of *Scabiosa caucasica* 'Clive Greaves', produced lavishly throughout the summer, are lovely with the smaller roses.

Rosa 'Louise Odier'

Origin: France (Margottin) 1851
Height: 5ft/1.5m
Z: 5

This Bourbon is a shrub that produces exceptionally pretty double pink flowers recurrently throughout the season. Its buds are very handsome: fat little spheres, framed as they open in pointed sepals, and showing a rosy red colour. The flowers open in June, magnificent and very double, deep pink, 3in/8cm across, with a light but sweet scent. The petals in the centre of the flower are arranged in quarters, framed by a circle of backward-curving petals. When they are fully open, golden-yellow stamens are revealed at the centre, and the petals become silver-pink with age. The flowers are borne in profuse weighty clusters, and further flowerings appear later in the season. In character they are a curious and attractive blend of the blowsy and the demure. It is a strong-growing healthy plant with bold shapely leaves.

A shrub rose with distinguished flowers borne recurrently throughout the season is very valuable. Plant 'Louise Odier' in a bold hot-coloured border where its rich pink flowers will harmonise with deep reds (for example the almost black-red flowers of *Potentilla atrosanguinea* – a marvellous combination) and plants with more violet-blue in their colouring, such as lavender or *Viola cornuta*. The tall lilac spires of *Veronicastrum virginicum* make a beautiful background.

Rosa 'Macrantha'

Origin: Europe
Height: 5ft/1.5m
Z: 6

Nobody knows exactly where this rose comes from, but despite its wild character it appears to be of garden origin, possibly a hybrid between the two European wild roses, *R. canina* and *R. gallica*. Its elegant little buds, tipped with pointed sepals, show a warm pink before the flowers open. The flowers in late May or June are single, creamy white, 2 1/2in/6cm across, with a very sweet scent. The petals are heart-shaped, silky in texture, and the centre of the flower is ornamentd with a bold tuft of deep golden-yellow stamens. The foliage has elegant little toothed leaflets with a shining surface. New growth is made in arching well-thorned stems. Spherical red hips are produced in late summer.

Rosa 'Macrantha' forms a dense, very vigorous, low-growing thicket, often twice as wide as it is high. Its essential quality lies in the contrast between its extraordinarily delicate flowers and its wild unrestrained habit of growth. It is a superb sight in full flower, wafting its lovely scent across the garden. It is no plant for a border. Plant it on a steep slope in a wilder corner of the garden, where it will sprawl downwards in a most decorative fashion.

Rosa 'Madame Delaroche-Lambert'

Origin: France (Robert) 1851
Height: 5ft/1.5m
Z: 5

This is one of the very best of the Moss roses – distinguished and decorative in every way. The mossy buds, which also have ornate pointed sepals, are carried aloft on talls stems clad in red-brown moss. The flowers, which open in June, are double, 3in/8cm across, a vibrant crimson-magenta – a wonderful colour. The form of the flower is slightly cupped but it opens out into an almost flat shape. The petals at the centre are folded and crimped, those at the edges curl backwards. The flowers are sweetly scented. The foliage is pale green, with shapely toothed leaves. It forms a vigorous upright bush. After the first summer flowering it will flower repeatedly throughout the season.

The brilliant flowers, held high on a bold shrub, make this a distinctly glamorous rose. In a scheme of reds and purples few roses would have a more telling effect. The purple in its colour, especially the lilac-purple of its fading petals, looks wonderful with lavender colours. The bold spires of meadow clary, *Salvia pratensis*, make a dazzling accompaniment. The silver-grey of some of the larger wormwoods, such as *Artemisia absinthium* – which has a hint of blue in its colouring – provides an especially beautiful background to the crimson flowers.

Rosa 'Madame Hardy'

Origin: France 1832
Height: 6ft/1.8m
Z: 4

'Madame Hardy' is a Damask, and one of the most beautiful of all garden plants; from the moment that its buds take shape in the late spring its distinction becomes apparent. The buds are globular, pink and encased in elaborate frilly sepals. The flowers open in June, double, 3in/8cm across, white but with undertones of cream and pink becoming more pronounced towards the centre. The petals are beautiful: undulating, creased and overlapping, with rounded ends. At the centre, framed in a ruff of smaller petals, there is a curious pale green eye. The scent is musky and sweet and the foliage is pale green. New growth has a pink flush and is covered in very fine hair-like thorns. All in all it is one of the most exquisite of roses.

Any plant quite so perfect as 'Madame Hardy' – big, upright, with distinguished foliage as well as its fabulous flowers – will show up the shortcomings, and especially the coarseness, of its neighbours. Plant it in a big mixed border to associate superbly with plants with cream or soft pink flowers – such as the creamy yellow *Sisyrinchium striatum*, creamy buff-flowered foxgloves such as *Digitalis × mertonensis*, and the pink-flowered cistus 'Peggy Sammons'. It flowers once only but for a good long period. Plant it, too, in a partially shaded place, where it looks especially beautiful.

Rosa 'Madame Isaac Pereire'

Origin: France (Garon) 1880
Height: 9ft/2.75m
Z: 5

This great Bourbon is one of the very best of the large-flowered shrub roses, with spectacular – and superlatively scented – flowers. Very plump buds, showing deep red through the green, open in June into sumptuous flowers, quartered, double, crimson-purple, at least 4in/10cm across. There is a second, late summer flowering when the flowers are said to be more perfectly formed than the earlier ones. The scent is rich, deep, sweet and powerful – among the finest of any rose. The foliage has especially bold, rounded, toothed leaflets up to 4in/10cm long

It perhaps makes more sense to think of 'Madame Isaac Pereire' as a climber than as a shrub, for it will in any case need support: the weight of the great flowers will cause the long stems to bow down. If given such support, it looks excellent at the back of a grand border, but this means that the scent is rather far away. Trained over a pergola, or forming a canopy for a bench, the delicious scent will be more easily savoured, and the

heavy flowers, seen from below, will be displayed to great effect, with the light shining through the rich purple. Or plant it as an immensely distinguished punctuation mark at either end of a long border, trained on a wooden tripod.

Rosa 'Madame Lauriol de Barny'

Origin: France (Trouillard) 1868
Height: 6ft/1.8m
Z: 5

This large Bourbon has particularly elegant pink flowers, and its buds have finely pointed sepals which part to show a cheerful red. The flowers, opening in June, are very beautiful: generously double, cupped, 3in/8cm across, borne in generous nodding clusters at the tips of branches. Their scent is marvellous – rich and sweet – and the colour a lovely mixture of rich pink within and a contrasting silver-pink on the reverse and towards the tips of the petals. After the first lavish burst of flowers in June it will produce a few flowers from time to time later in the season.

'Madame Lauriol de Barny' has rather lax growth, throwing out long slender stems. In smaller gardens, where space may be limited, train it as a climber in a position of importance; its exquisite, richly scented flowers, borne repeatedly throughout the season, will make a wonderful ornament. In a border it will need support: train it up a pillar or wooden tripod to make a spectacular feature. The warm pink of its flowers is marvellously effective with blue – either the pale to mid blue of sage (*Salvia officinalis*, particularly good in its purple-leafed form), or the deeper violet-blue of the larger campanulas (such as *C. lactiflora* which will rise almost as high as the rose).

Rosa 'Madame Legras de Saint Germain'

Origin: France before 1848
Height: 6ft/1.8m
Z: 4

This Alba is equally good as a substantial shrub or, in the smaller garden, trained as a climber. Its pointed buds are fringed with decorative sepals and they open in June to double creamy white flowers, 2 1/2in/6cm across, with a fine musky scent. The flowers are very neat flat rosettes when first open but as they age they become much blowsier. The petals have a silken texture, with scalloped tips, and fold and undulate in a lively way. The grey-green foliage has elegant toothed leaflets.

'Madame Legras de Saint Germain' will form a tall, distinguished free-standing shrub, its creamy white flowers looking splendid against the grey-green foliage. Grown in this way it would be superb as part of the essential structure of a grand border, for although it flowers only once the foliage is a continuing ornament, giving an excellent background to other plantings. Because its new growth is long and whippy it can also be trained very successfully as a climber, when it looks wonderful festooned with the off-white flowers of the clematis 'Alba Luxurians' in late summer.

Rosa 'Madame Pierre Oger'

Origin: France (Verdier) 1878
Height: 4ft/1.2m
Z: 5

This lovely Bourbon is a sport of 'Reine Victoria', and the flowers are very similar – double, cupped, sweetly scented – though the colour of 'Madame Pierre Oger' is much paler, a very distinguished delicate silver-pink, slightly deeper within. The petals are very faintly mottled in deeper pink, with decorative, slightly frilly edges. The flowers are quite small, 2in/5cm across, starting in June but with repeat flowerings later in the season, and are carried in very generous clusters on upright stems. The foliage has shapely, slightly toothed and pointed leaflets, and unfortunately shares 'Reine Victoria's' susceptibility to black spot.

The beautiful flowers and air of distinction determine the quality of this rose. Delicacy, airiness and refinement are the essential attributes of related plantings. Avoid, above all, adjacent plantings of anything coarse or overblown – their defects will be made even more apparent. Plant instead such things as the smaller campanulas, cistus, geraniums, irises and sages. I have seen 'Madame Pierre Oger' looking splendid rising above mounds of *Santolina pinnata* ssp. *neapolitana* with its very pale silver-grey foliage (cut off its rather horribly strident yellow flowers in bud, and clip it over to give it a good rounded shape).

Rosa 'Madame Plantier'

Origin: France (Plantier) 1835
Height: 8ft/2.5m
Z: 4

This rose is usually grouped among the Albas but its origins are uncertain. It has very ornamental buds fringed with ornate pointed sepals which part to show rosy red. The flowers, starting in June, are double, white with a creamy centre, 3in/8cm across. They have none of the crisp neatness of the characteristic Albas but are composed of curving and folded petals, of a silky texture, which form an attractively muddled, rather loose flower. It is perfumed with a light but sweet scent. The foliage is pale green with toothed leaflets. Flowers are carried in generous clusters on long stems.

'Madame Plantier' has very beautiful flowers and forms a rather lax bush which has none of the typically statuesque presence of the true Alba. It will flower well in partial shade, and is often trained as a climber when it will rise to at least twice its height as a bush. As a free-standing shrub in the border it really needs some sort of artificial support; it makes a very striking feature trained on a tripod, rising above mixed plantings. Its creamy white flowers will harmonise with almost any scheme – plant it with waves of *Sisyrinchium striatum*, white foxgloves, *Digitalis purpurea albiflora*, or its creamy yellow-flowered perennial cousin, *D. grandiflora*.

Rosa 'Madame Zöetmans'

Origin: France (Marest) 1830
Height: 4ft/1.2m
Z: 4

This distinguished old Damask is especially recommended for the smaller garden. When the pointed sepals first separate, the half-open buds show a decorative salmon-pink. The fully open flowers in June are double, 3in/8cm across, the palest creamy pink, becoming whiter as they age but always retaining a flush of pink. They have a marvellous sweet scent. The petals are strikingly arranged, at first in a loosely quartered pattern but later swirling hither and thither round the edge and gathered in a neat button at the centre, eventually revealing a green eye. The foliage is handsome, with pale green toothed leaves.

'Madame Zöetmans' has exceptionally beautiful, well scented flowers on a compact bush. But the flowering shoots are rather lax and need support. The colour of its flowers allows it to mix harmoniously with either a pale scheme or something livelier. It looks superb with an underplanting of *Geranium* × *oxonianum* 'Claridge Druce' whose warm pink flowers will appear before those of the rose and continue throughout the season. It is equally at home with much stronger reds such as the cheerful red of *Potentilla* 'Gibson's Scarlet' whose trailing flowering stems will intermingle with the rose.

Rosa 'Marchesa Boccella'

Origin: France (Moreau-Robert) 1868
Height: 36in/90cm
Z: 4

'Marchesa Boccella' was widely known under the name 'Jacques Cartier'. It is a small Portland rose with all the presence of the larger old shrub roses in a compact form. Striking plump red buds, with very long pointed sepals, open in June to tightly packed double flowers, 3in/8cm across, warm pink in colour. Cupped at first, the flowers open out fully into sumptuous rosettes, carried in generous clusters and giving off a rich sweet scent. The petals are tightly packed in the centre, in a vaguely quartered arrangement, but those at the edges curve backwards, forming an elegant frame. The leaves are an excellent fresh green, boldly shaped and toothed, with a pronounced pattern of veins. New growth bristles with fine red hair-like thorns. It repeat flowers very well.

'Marchesa Boccella' forms a vigorous upright little bush and, with its repeat flowering, is an ideal shrub rose for the smaller garden. Plant it in a modest mixed border with geraniums, lavender, the purple-leafed sage, *Salvia officinalis* 'Purpurascens' and the silver-blue shimmering flowers of perennial flax, *Linum perenne*. At the edge of a terrace it will perfume the air and give ornament throughout the season. A pair planted in pots makes a lovely ornament to the top of a flight of steps. It flowers very well in the shade and is especially valuable for town gardens.

Rosa 'Marguerite Hilling'

Origin: Britain (Hilling)
1959
Height: 8ft/2.5m
Z: 5

This is a sport of 'Nevada' (described below), which it resembles in every way except in its flowers. Its buds are long and pointed and when the sepals part they show a warm red. The flowers in late May or June are an excellent lively blush pink, fading towards white in the centre. The petals fold and curve more wildly than in 'Nevada', giving the flowers as they age a splendidly voluptuous air. As they age they also become much paler, showing a mottled veining.

In full flow, 'Marguerite Hilling' is a wonderful sight, covered in billowing, sweetly-scented pink

Illustration opposite:
Rosa 'Mary Rose'

flowers. Like 'Nevada', this huge rose is very much a plant for a wild place in the garden, though it will also make a major contribution in early summer to a very large border, where its grey-green foliage will provide an especially good background to lively reds and rich purples of other plants later in the summer. One of the dramatic red clematis of late summer, such as the beautiful single-flowered *C. viticella* 'Abundance', would look marvellous climbing through it.

Rosa 'Mary Rose'

Origin: Britain (Austin)
1983
Height: 4ft/1.2m
Z: 5

This David Austin introduction, with double pink flowers, is a splendid perpetual-flowering shrub of compact size. It has big buds tipped with pointed sepals which separate to show bright red. The half-open flower is beautifully formed, scrolled, with curving outer petals. The flowers, which open fully in June, are lavishly double, an excellent pink, pale but warm, 4in/10cm across, with a good sweet scent. The flowers have much of the style of the old shrub roses, with loosely gathered petals turning the palest silvery pink as they age. They are carried in very generous clusters on upright stems. The foliage is excellent: bold shapely dark leaflets have a shining surface and emphatically marked veins.

'Mary Rose' makes a vigorous neat bush and produces its very ornamental flowers throughout the season. It has far more personality than the vast majority of perpetual-flowering modern roses. Plant it in a mixed border and it will be one of the best performers, giving colour and character over a very long season. It is one of the best roses for the smaller garden, and does well in a pot: a pair, on a terrace flanking a garden door, for example, would make a lovely ornament.

Rosa 'Mevrouw Nathalie Nypels'

Origin: Netherlands
(Leenders) 1919
Height: 36in/90cm
Z: 5

Also known as *R.* 'Nathalie Nypels', this is a Floribunda which has much more character, and more charm, than most others in this group. It starts to flower in June, and at first the double flowers are

elegantly cupped, an excellent warm pink. When they open fully they are loosely double, 3in/8cm across, with undulating petals covered in a fine network of veins in a deeper colour and an occasional vague stripe of white. They have a marvellous intensely sweet scent, and will continue to be produced throughout the season. The leaves are boldly shaped, a rich dark green with a shining surface. It makes a neat compact bush.

'Mevrouw Nathalie Nypels' is in many respects the ideal rose for the smaller garden or for a position at the front in a large border. Its colouring is emphatic without being overpowering and its generous clusters of flowers will make a strong contribution to a mixed planting. Its small size means that lower-growing plants with trailing growth, such as the smaller geraniums and *Viola cornuta*, can decoratively intermingle. I have also seen it used very effectively in a mixed planting in a pot with the lovely rich blue trailing *Convolvulus sabatius*.

Rosa moyesii

Origin: Western China (1894)
Height: 10ft/3m
Z: 5

Every garden, if there is the space, should include this stately wild rose – one of the largest and loveliest of all shrub roses. Its buds are almost spherical with a ruff of thorns at the base; as the sepals part, the petals appear black-red. The flowers, in June, are slightly less dark but still a beautiful blood-red, single, 2 1/2in/6cm across. At first they are delicately cupped, but when

Illustration: *Rosa moyesii* 'Geranium'

fully open are quite flat, the heart-shaped petals overlapping slightly. At the centre of the flower, decorative stamens are gold and black like the frogging on a dress military uniform. The foliage is an elegant grey-green with rounded and slightly toothed leaflets. Lastly, and perhaps the most beautiful feature of the plant, the hips in August are spectacular: at least 1 1/2in/4cm long, flask-shaped, bright red and retaining a tuft of twisting sepals. Since many plants raised from seed are supposedly sterile and will thus be deprived of the marvellous hips, and since some clones have better darker flowers than others, make sure when buying a plant that it has been propagated from cuttings from a good clone. *R. m.* 'Geranium' with geranium-red flowers and *R. m.* 'Sealing Wax' with pink flowers and very large hips are good cultivars.

Although it is possible to use *R. moyesii* in a very large border, where its great arching stems will sway, covered in flowers, above other plantings, it is much too big and too wild for such a tame position in most gardens. In a woodland garden, with other large shrubs, set in roughly mown grass, it will be at its very best. It flowers happily in a fairly shady position.

Rosa 'Mrs Doreen Pike'

Origin: Britain (Austin) 1993
Height: 36in/90cm
Z: 4

This new Rugosa is an excellent example of the vitality of a particular group of roses and the skills of modern rose breeding. The buds have the full Rugosa charm: they are long, flask-shaped and slightly hairy, with slender sepals extending far beyond the tip of the bud. As they open the sepals spread out widely and a lovely pale pink is revealed. The flowers, in June, are double, 3in/8cm across, with a mass of petals the texture of crumpled silk. The colour is a mixture of cerise-pink and silver-pink, with a green-yellow eye at the centre. They have a sweet musky scent. Like other Rugosas it is recurrent flowering. The foliage is beautiful: gleaming pale green with folded and toothed leaflets. It forms a wide mound with spreading side growth. It will flower well in the semi-shade.

'Mrs Doreen Pike' seems to be bursting with vigour. New growth, bearing many buds, erupts from the bush. The pink flowers look marvellous against the healthy, shining leaves. It is an ideal plant for the front of the border where its trailing side growth will happily intermingle with smaller plants. It would also, with much feeding and watering, be marvellous cascading over the brim of a substantial pot.

Rosa 'Mrs John Laing'

Origin: Britain (Bennett) 1887
Height: 4ft/1.2m
Z: 5

'Mrs John Laing' is a splendid Hybrid Perpetual with beautiful shapely flowers. It was bred by Henry Bennett who raised the very first Hybrid Teas in the 1870s. Its buds have tufts of pointed sepals which separate to reveal a rich red, and the half-opened flower is exquisitely scrolled. The flowers in June are double, elegant, pale silver-pink, 3in/8cm across, and perfumed with a rich sweet scent. The centre of the flower remains cupped, while the outer petals curve backwards, and the flower are borne in clusters well aloft on long stems. The foliage is a handsome mid green, rounded and toothed. After the main summer flowering it will flower repeatedly throughout the season.

This is an exceptionally vigorous, healthy rose. With its bushy upright shape and profusion of very decorative flowers it would be a key plant in a mixed border. It associates well with blues and violets, and because of its long flowering period there are many opportunities for happy companion planting. Plant it with the campanulas, lavenders and sages of high summer, and the caryopteris, perovskia and sky-blue *Salvia uliginosa* of late summer. I have seen it looking beautiful in early August surrounded by waves of white Japanese anemone (*Anemone* × *hybrida* 'Honorine Jobert').

Rosa 'Mrs William Paul'

Origin: Britain (Paul) 1869
Height: 36in/90cm
Z: 5

This Moss rose has all sorts of decorative virtues but for some reason is not at all well known. Its mossy buds, dusty red in colour, open in June to lavish, very double warm pink flowers 3 1/2in/9cm across. The petals are densely packed but they form shapely flowers. The texture of the petals is attractive, and they are slightly mottled with a paler silver-pink. The

Illustration opposite:
Rosa 'Nevada'

flowers have a warm spicy scent and after the main flowering will flower recurrently throughout the season. The foliage is leaden green with rather leathery toothed leaflets; new growth is flushed with bronze. Flowers are carried in generous clusters, jostling for room at the tips of very thorny new growth, rising well above the foliage.

'Mrs William Paul' is a vigorous healthy rose with lavish, richly decorative flowers. As a garden plant it is very versatile. In a grand border it will make a bold contribution to a scheme of pinks, blues and mauves. In a smaller border it could be a key structural plant, both for its recurrent flowers and its handsome foliage. The grey in its foliage colour gives it special affinity with lavender, sage and the perennial wallflower *Erysimum* 'Bowles Mauve' whose perpetual flowers will also associate well with the rose. Plant it also in pots; it makes a marvellous terrace ornament in a small garden.

Rosa 'Nevada'

Origin: Spain (Dot) 1927
Height: 8ft/2.5m
Z: 5

There is much argument about the parentage of this great rose – is it a form of *R. moyesii* or of *R. pimpinellifolia*? It certainly has a splendid wild character. It starts to flower in May, when large cone-shaped yellow buds open into semi-double flowers. These are at first slightly cupped, creamy yellow, with glowing lemon-yellow stamens at the centre. When they open fully they are 4in/10cm across,

a lovely cream colour, with a striking tuft of stamens. Slightly twisting petals give a greater fullness to the flower, and some older flowers are slightly flecked with pink. After the first lavish early summer flowering, intermittent flowers may be produced throughout the season, with another flush in late summer. They have only a slight scent. The foliage has much of the character of wild roses; it is grey-green, with rounded and slightly toothed leaflets. New growth is a striking chocolate-brown in colour, with boldly arching stems. Some gardeners say that flowering in older bushes is improved by the comprehensive pruning of old wood.

'Nevada' forms a big vigorous shrub and flowers with the most spectacular abandon, covering the bush with creamy white. When in flower there are few more splendid garden plants. I have seen 'Nevada' used very effectively at the back of a substantial border where its flowers are big enough, and its habit sufficiently imposing, to give it tremendous presence even at a distance. It is equally at home in a woodland garden, where few shrubs will outshine it. Plant it, for example, as a superb eye-catcher at the end of a grassy walk.

Rosa 'Nuits de Young'

Origin: France (Laffay) 1845
Height: 4ft/1.2m
Z: 5

This Moss rose was formerly known as 'Old Black' – a reference to its most striking quality, the very deep colour of its flowers. The buds are only slightly mossed and the flowers which open in June are striking dark

crimson rosettes 2in/5cm across. The petals curve
backwards and forwards, occasionally revealing paler
undersides, and their texture is that of old velvet. As
they get older they become blowsier and fade to an
attractive lilac-purple, when the yellow stamens also
become visible. The scent of the flowers is exceptional
– a fabulous deep almost tropical perfume. The foliage
is a good dark green. It forms a strongly growing bush
with rather upright growth; the flowering stems,
covered in fine red hair-like thorns, are held high.

The very dark colour, relatively small but intricate
flowers and exceptional scent are the most precious
qualities of this rose. It is essential to plant it where it
may be savoured close up. It will flower best, and
diffuse its scent most effectively, in a sunny position;
small beds on either side of a sitting place, with other
scented plants such as lavender, pinks or sage, would be
excellent. In a red and purple colour scheme it will add
a rich and sombre note.

Rosa nutkana 'Plena'

Origin: Western North
America, 1894
Height: 8ft/2.5m
Z: 5

This was formerly known as *R. californica* 'Plena'. In
all its detail, and in its whole appearance, it is a
marvellous rose. The buds are a decorative russet
colour and have long sepals, spreading far beyond the
tips. When first open they present elegantly scrolled
flowers; by early June these have fully opened out,

semi-double, rich pink, 2 1/2in/6cm across. They never become completely flat – the petals curve, separate and rise gently upwards, and the outer petals are a paler silver-pink, on which an intricate pattern of veins is clearly seen. They have a delicious scent, sweet and vibrant. The foliage is a fine grey-green with elegant little toothed leaflets; short flowering shoots contribute to the dense texture of the bush. The hips, which take on their colour in the summer, are melon-shaped and orange-red, retaining the pointed sepals which had been such a feature of the buds.

A mature bush of *R. nutkana* 'Plena' in full flower in June is one of the loveliest sights in a garden. It looks marvellous in a deep mixed border where its upright dense habit, attractive leaf-colour and decorative hips will be ornamental long after its flowering. I have grown it successfully in an orchard among apple trees, quinces and medlars, where its wild character made it entirely at home.

Rosa 'Nyveldt's White'

Origin: Netherlands (Nyveldt) 1955
Height: 5ft/1.5m
Z: 4

Some roses make an immediate dramatic impact, while others seduce gradually, revealing their charms over time. This lovely Rugosa is definitely of the latter kind. It has creamy pink cone-shaped buds embellished with whiskery sepals from which the flowers emerge in June. They are single, white, 3 1/2in/9cm across, with a striking tuft of lemon-yellow stamens. The petals are very elegant, undulating and silky; slightly overlapping, they are etched with a network of veins. The flowers have a light but sweet scent. The foliage is beautiful: it has the characteristic leathery shining leaves of Rugosas, but the leaflets are a lively green, longer and narrower, flopping slightly. It produces magnificent hips which start very early, even during the first flush of flowers, and in late summer turn a lovely scarlet.

This was, it is said, originally raised as a hedging rose, but its vigorous and upright growth, graceful flowers and distinguished foliage are much better suited to use as a free-standing plant. Grow it in a mixed border, where its recurrent flowers will give ornament throughout the season and associate well with almost any plant, or in some more informal setting where its bold but refined character will be appreciated. It flowers well in partial shade where it displays its glowing flowers and gleaming leaves to best advantage.

Rosa × *odorata* 'Mutabilis'

Origin: China before 1896
Height: 8ft/2.5m
Z: 7

This mysterious rose, of very uncertain origin, was formerly known as 'Tipo Ideale' (it first appeared in Italy) and as *R. turkestanica*. Its long pointed buds show an orange-red at first and open in June into big single flowers, 2 1/2in/6cm across. When they first open the flowers are slightly cupped, a pale apricot colour with hints of red. The flowers then become flat, with elegant well-separated petals, a warm crimson-pink, with a light sweet scent. After the first superb show of flowers it will flower constantly throughout the season. The foliage has small shapely leaflets attractively flushed with bronze when young.

There is an air of mystery about 'Mutabilis'. Some gardeners hate its changing colours. I find that I like it increasingly, the more I see of it. Whether or not you like the colours, the flowers are undeniably elegant and as they age the petals twist gracefully. It is fairly tender, but in a well protected garden will form a magnificent, broad spreading shrub of open habit. Its slender new growth may be trained very effectively, though it may need the protection of a wall. At Kiftsgate Court there is a magnificent specimen which climbs over 20ft/6m up a wall. Bold gardeners will use *R.* × *odorata* 'Mutabilis' as the dramatic centrepiece for some daring colour scheme. The more timid will plant it as a single specimen, alone and magnificent.

Rosa × *odorata* 'Pallida'

Origin: China 1789
Height: 6ft/1.8m
Z: 7

This old China rose goes under many different names. It is now correctly known as *R.* × *odorata* 'Pallida' but it was also known as 'Old Blush China', 'Parson's Pink' and as the 'Monthly Rose', from its ability to flower in any month of the year. It is historically an important rose because it is one of the 'four stud Chinas', the essential ancestors of countless modern roses. It is still a marvellous plant and well worth a place in any garden. Its rich pink buds open into double flowers, 2 1/2in/6cm across, a lovely silver-pink but veined with a deeper colour. The petals curl at the edges and form a very loosely shaped flower of irresistible charm. The scent is marvellous, intensely sweet and clear. Although it produces its chief burst of flowers in the summer, it is perpetual-flowering and may even produce flowers in mid winter. The leaves are elegantly shaped, rounded and coming to a fine point.

'Old Blush' will form an upright bush but may also successfully be trained on a sunny wall where it will have the best chance of flowering in winter. Used in this way, I think it is at its best alone, with nothing to detract from its subtle charm. But it is a good shrub for the mixed border where it should be used in association with similarly delicate and well-mannered plants. Its pink flowers go well with the silver-blue of herbaceous perennials such as *Campanula persicifolia* and, later in the season, with blue-flowered *Perovskia atriplicifolia* with its pale grey finely cut foliage.

Rosa 'Oeillet Parfait'

Origin: France (Foulard)
1841
Height: 4ft/1.2m
Z: 4

This is also known as 'Oeillet Flamand'. 'Oeillet' is the French for carnation and the flowers of this Damask, carried at the tips of tall stems, do resemble carnations or pinks. The buds are very ornamental, with intricate

pointed sepals parting to reveal the deep red of the unfolding bud. The flowers, which open in June, are a warm rich pink, 3in/8cm across, with a a delicious warm, spicy scent. They are borne in lavish clusters at the tips of stems that bristle with very fine red thorns. The petals swirl hither and thither but are tightly packed, giving the flowers an attractive neat shape. The foliage has pleated leaflets, with an emphatic pattern of veins, and the leaves are appealingly floppy, fluttering in the breeze. New growth is thin and rather lax, and may need support; it should be pruned after flowering to encourage strong new growth.

This cheerful well scented rose will fit in harmoniously with many different kinds of planting. Use it, of course, in a bed of pinks – white, parti-coloured and pink – where, quite apart from the reference to the rose's name, it looks beautiful. In a border the best way to give it the support it needs is by planting it close alongside sympathetic small shrubs such as *Cistus ladanifer* with white flowers and a crimson spot at the centre, or the lavender *Lavandula angustifolia* 'Munstead' with pale blue flowers.

Rosa 'Paulii'

Origin: Britain (Paul) 1903
Height: 4ft/1.2m
Z: 4

This is a cross between *R. rugosa* and the northern European field rose, *R. arvensis*. It has long pointed creamy buds with very striking pointed sepals that stick out well beyond the tip of the bud. The flowers, which open in June, are single, white, 4in/10cm across,

with very prominent egg-yellow stamens and a delicious sweet scent. The petals in the mature flower are separate, rounded at the tips, slightly folded and with the texture of softly crushed silk. They are dazzlingly beautiful. The foliage is an excellent mid green in colour, with strongly marked veins. It will form a very wide sprawling bush, two or three times as wide as it is high. The growth is very dense, with a profusion of prickly stems, and it acts as a splendid weed suppressant. There is a beautiful pink-flowered form, *R.* 'Paulii Rosea', which is said to grow less vigorously and to produce a second flowering later in the season.

The flowers and foliage of *R.* 'Paulii' have all the character of a wild rose, and its habit of growth makes it one of the finest of all ground-cover plants. It is at its best in the informal parts of the garden: in a shrubbery or orchard, for example, or on a sloping site, down which it will pour its cascade of flowers. It will do perfectly well in shade and it would magnificently fill a substantial corner in a yard or between outhouses.

Rosa 'Pax'

Origin: Britain
(Pemberton) 1918
Height: 6ft/1.8m
Z: 4

This is one of the very best recurrent-flowering white roses. Its long pointed buds are very decorative, with whiskery sepals. As the sepals part, the flower colour appears creamy yellow, but when the flowers open in June they are a dazzling white with cream shadows at the centre. They are very loosely double, gently cupped, 4in/10cm across, and have a sweet and lovely scent. They open out more fully as they age, revealing golden-yellow stamens. The first flowers are very profusely carried on the tips of old growth; later flowerings, equally lavish, occur on the fleshy new stems that erupt from the bush. The new growth is a striking red-brown and the leaves are boldly toothed, shapely and exceptionally large – up to 4in/10cm long.

'Pax', despite its crisply demure name, has a voluptuous character. Its softly curving petals, loose informal shape and large and languid foliage give it an air of abandon. Its habit is rather lax, too, and it needs support; indeed, it can be trained very effectively as a climbing rose. In a big border, train it up a tripod or

Illustration opposite:
Rosa 'Penelope'

obelisk where it will make a dramatic eye-catcher, flowering throughout the season. If left to its own devices it will straggle and climb through neighbouring plants in an extremely effective way. As a chief ingredient in a mixed planting of pale colours 'Pax' is exceptionally valuable.

Rosa 'Penelope'

Origin: Britain
(Pemberton) 1924
Height: 6ft/1.8m
Z: 5

This Hybrid Musk has many virtues and is an excellent example of the art of the rose breeder; remote in appearance from its wild ancestry, it nonetheless completely lacks that artificiality that spoils so many modern roses. Its buds have decorative sepals, long and pointed, which when they part reveal a vivid orange-pink. But when the flowers open in early June they are a warm pink at the centre, fading white at the edges. They are loosely double, 3 1/2in/9cm across, and have a sweet and spicy scent. As the flowers age they become almost white and the petals, crimped and curling at the edges, separate even further, giving a greater fullness to the flower. The leaves are dark green, boldly toothed and rounded, and the new growth is a handsome red-brown. 'Penelope' will produce flowers throughout the season, to be followed in autumn by curious and decorative hips: glistening little pale pink berries.

In a slightly shady place, where it will flower well, the special charms of 'Penelope' are best revealed. In a cooler and less sunlit position the colour and form of the flowers will change more slowly. It is a marvellous border plant; its lavish flowering and striking character – generous and abundant rather than neat and formal – give a powerful flavour. It will hold its own, in an unaggressive way, with almost any plant.

Rosa 'Perle des Panachées'

Origin: France (Vibert)
1845
Height: 36in/90cm
Z: 5

Of all the roses with parti-coloured flowers this is one of the best. It has beautiful buds – fat, blood-red and framed in pointed sepals. They open in June into double flowers, 2 1/2in/6cm across, creamy white but striped and splashed irregularly with vivid carmine.

Although the flowers are compact and neatly formed, the petals point in different directions, following no pattern, which gives them a lively appearance. The scent is musky, light but distinct. Pale green leaves have deeply marked veins and a leathery texture.

'Perle des Panachées' forms a neat, vigorous, upright little bush. The contrast between the neatly shaped flower and the lively arrangement of sprightly coloured petals is especially attractive. It is an excellent small rose to plant towards the front of a border. With your associated planting, keep things airy and insubstantial – simple plants like pale mauve *Viola cornuta*, the smaller-flowered geraniums (such as the pale rose-pink *G. endressii* 'Wargrave Pink') or *Astrantia major* 'Rubra' are the right kinds of things.

Rosa 'Petite de Hollande'

Origin: Netherlands before 1800
Height: 36in/90cm
Z: 5

Also known as 'Pompon des Dames', this little Centifolia rose has many of the virtues of the larger shrub roses, in a compact form. The buds, carried in profuse clusters at the tips of new growth, have very ornamental sepals, elaborate and pointed, extending far beyond the tip of the bud. The flowers in June, 2in/5cm across, are very double, a lively rose-carmine, turning silver at the edges, and very sweetly scented. The flowers are slightly cupped when they first open and when fully open the petals swirl hither and thither in a lively way. As the flowers age the colour becomes a pale silvery pink. The foliage is pinnate, a slightly glaucous-green, and the leaflets are pleated and toothed. The pale green new growth is strikingly covered in fine hair-like thorns.

'Petite de Hollande', free-flowering and deliciously scented, is especially valuable because of its compact size. It makes a vigorous little bush, and foliage and flowers are in proportion to its size. Plant it in a sunny position in a little mixed border surrounded by plants of comparable delicacy: violet and white *Viola cornuta*, *Nigella damascena* (particularly the more double-flowered cultivar 'Miss Jekyll') and silver-grey *Stachys byzantina* have the right qualities.

Rosa 'Petite Lisette'

Origin: France (Vibert) 1817
Height: 4ft/1.2m
Z: 4

'Petite Lisette' is one of the smaller Damask roses but has all the character of her larger sisters. The buds are strikingly ornamental, fringed with elaborate sepals like Gothic tracery. The buds open in June to form double rosettes, 2 1/2in/6cm across, pale pink but with a hint of mauve, paling to silver-pink at the edge. The petals overlap attractively and at the centre they are grouped in a whorl, framing the stamens. The flower heads are held well up at the tips of finely thorned stems. They are deliciously perfumed with a deep sweet scent. The foliage is mid green with rounded toothed leaflets.

The exceptional quality of 'Petite Lisette' is delicacy, making it one of the best smaller shrub roses for gardens of modest size. The small flowers are perfectly in proportion to the size of the plant and sway prettily at the tips of slender new growth. It is excellent towards the front of a border in a position where its lovely scent may be savoured. Underplant it with pinks which, apart from the beauty of their flowers and perfume, have pale grey foliage that makes an excellent foil for roses. It looks beautiful with cushions of the narrow-leafed sage, *Salvia lavandulifolia*, or with the shimmering, silvery blue flowers of the perennial flax, *Linum perenne*.

Illustration: Rosa pimpinellifolia 'Grandiflora'

Rosa pimpinellifolia

Origin: Northern Europe
Height: 36in/90cm
Z: 4

The Scotch, or Burnet rose, found growing in sandy places, often by the sea-shore, is one of the loveliest of European wild roses. The species makes a low-growing shrub with little yellow buds that open in May to extremely elegant little cupped flowers, 1 1/2in/4cm, across, usually creamy white but occasionally pink. The foliage is very decorative and fern-like, with grey-green toothed leaflets. The growth is very prickly, and striking black hips are produced in late summer. It is

Illustration: *Rosa* ×
harisonii

one of the hardiest of all roses and will flourish in very
poor soil.

There are many cultivars and hybrids of
R. pimpinellifolia that make admirable garden plants.
Most of them are quite small and a collection would
make a most attractive feature in a small garden. There
are many more than those that I list here. The
'Dunwich Rose' forms a striking mound, about
24in/60cm high and at least twice as wide, with profuse
creamy yellow single flowers, 1 1/2in/4cm across, of
exquisite beauty. It is a very healthy plant and an
excellent rose of small size but wild character for a
town garden. Although flowering once only it has very
decorative foliage, with little pleated leaflets, and it
makes a shapely bush. A large-flowered cultivar,
R. pimpinellifolia 'Grandiflora' (also known as
R. p. altaica) has much bigger flowers than the type,
2 1/2in/6cm across, creamy white and very graceful,
with prominent yellow stamens and a golden centre. It
makes a much more substantial bush, up to 5ft/1.5m
high. It is a superlative late spring-flowering rose and
will flower well in the shade. *R. p.* 'Harisonii' (now
known correctly as *R.*× *harisonii*, or 'Harison's
Yellow'), has beautiful glowing yellow flowers, at first
globe-shaped but opening out into semi-double flowers
2in/5cm across. It makes a leggy bush, with especially
handsome grey foliage, up to 6ft/1.8m high. It flowers
well in the shade. Use it in some wild place in the
garden – perhaps to follow on after daffodils.

Rosa 'Pompon Blanc Parfait'

Origin: 1876
Height: 5ft/1.5m
Z: 4

This is one of the smaller Albas, with beautiful flowers and a very long flowering season. Plump hairy buds, with pointed, intricate sepals, open in June to double flowers, 2 1/2in/6cm across. Despite its name, the flowers are far from perfectly white – they are suffused with a very pale creamy pink. The petals swirl about in the centre but at the edges they are arranged in neat concentric circles, curving elegantly backwards. The flowers are carried in lavish clusters and are held high on the almost thornless pale green new growth. They have an excellent scent – rich and deep. The foliage is grey-green, with toothed leaves rather smaller than in other Albas.

'Pompon Blanc Parfait' has all the best qualities of the Alba roses – upright growth, handsome foliage and beautiful flowers – but in a more compact form, making it the perfect member of the group for smaller gardens. Its emphatic shape, and flowers that harmonise easily, allow many uses in the garden. A pair flanking an entrance, or the opening of a path, look beautiful. It will also make an admirable structural plant in a border, and especially in an arrangement of pale colours – blues, pinks, creams and soft whites – where it looks wonderful.

Rosa 'Portlandica'

Origin: Italy before 1775
Height: 36in/90cm
Z: 4

Often referred to as the Portland Rose or 'Duchess of Portland', this is an early hybrid of *R. gallica* that is still a very attractive garden rose. Striking purple buds are fringed with pointed sepals, and open in June into semi-double flowers, 3in/8cm across, a sprightly purple-pink in colour, with an excellent spicy scent. The petals are frilled at the edges, veined in a deeper colour and at the centre a ruff of smaller petals surrounds the golden stamens. As the flower ages it becomes a silver-pink. The foliage has pale green toothed and pleated leaflets. If regularly deadheaded it will produce flowers throughout the season.

This is a valuable small shrub rose. Its flowers are well held in generous clusters above handsome foliage. The lively colour of the flowers is well displayed against the pale foliage. It suckers freely and will make an admirable and ornamental low hedge on either side of a path, where its rich perfume can be savoured to the full. It is also good in a border with a colour scheme of reds, pinks and purples, and is low enough to make an excellent companion for the smaller herbaceous plants: diascias, smaller geraniums, pinks and violas that make such good front-of-the-border plants. Some of the lower-growing shrubs, such as sages, also look good with it; *Salvia officinalis* 'Purpurascens' makes a lovely partner.

Rosa 'Président de Sèze'

Origin: France (Hébert)
1836
Height: 5ft/1.5m
Z: 4

'Président de Sèze', also known as 'Madame Hébert' and as 'Jenny Duval', is a Gallica with spectacular flowers of a distinctive colour. The buds, carried on very finely thorned stems, are especially beautiful: almost spherical, framed in lacy sepals which twist back decoratively to reveal the deep red of the bud. The flowers open in June, double, rich magenta-pink, 3in/8cm across, packed with petals at the centre and with outer petals a paler silver and curving backwards. As the flowers age they become more muddled in form, and the colour turns to a marvellous faded lilac-purple. They have an excellent sweet musky scent. The foliage has bold pale green leaflets that arch backwards.

Beautiful flowers, good scent and distinction of foliage all commend 'Président de Sèze'. It forms a fine upright, very floriferous bush and altogether has a striking presence. Use it in a mixed border; the bold flowers will give drama but their colour will harmonise easily with both paler pinks and deeper purples. It also looks excellent with flowers on the mauve side of blue, such as *Campanula persicifolia* or the tall spires of field sage, *Salvia pratensis*. I have also seen it looking very beautiful planted on the edge of a lawn on which its falling petals, pale violet-pink, were scattered.

Rosa 'Prince Charles'

Origin: Unknown, before 1918
Height: 4ft/1.2m
Z: 5

This Bourbon has spectacular, very deep purple flowers, unlike those of any other rose in its group. When the sepals encasing the buds start to separate they reveal almost black blood-red petals within. The flowers, opening in June, are at first slightly cupped, double, 3in/8cm across, a very deep crimson-purple in colour, and perfumed with a sweet musky scent. The petals curl backwards and their very edges have a hint of silver-purple. As the flowers age they become much more loosely double, with petals curving backwards to reveal prominent golden stamens, and the colour fades to red-magenta. The flowers are carried well above the foliage, borne on tall stems of very pale green, bristling with red hair-like thorns. Unlike some of the other Bourbons, 'Prince Charles' flowers only once. The boldly shaped leaves are an unusual pale green with deeply marked veins.

The colour of the flowers gives 'Prince Charles' its particular distinction. It will flower well in partial shade, although I have seen it beautifully used in a sunny border among the slender purple leaves of *Lobelia × speciosa* 'Queen Victoria' and the swaying crimson flower heads of *Knautia macedonica*. It makes a rather lax bush which would benefit from the support of smaller shrubs like lavender or *Caryopteris × clandonensis*, whose lead-grey foliage makes an excellent foil to the crimson flowers of the rose.

Rosa 'Raubritter'

Origin: Germany (Kordes) 1936
Height: 36in/90cm
Z: 4

This modern rose, a hybrid of *R.* 'Macrantha', has an unusual habit of growth and striking flowers. It starts to flower in June, producing a profusion of cupped semi-double flowers carried in clusters, 2in/5cm across, with a prominent bush of stamens and with a light sweet scent. The flowers remain cupped, like some miniature Bourbon rose, a lively, rich pink at first but fading to a soft silver-pink. When the plant is covered in flowers this variation in colour creates a shimmering effect. Although flowering only once it does so for a long period. The dark foliage has neat, slightly toothed leaflets with strongly marked veins and the new growth bristles with fine thorns.

The cheerful but elegant flowers are allied in 'Raubritter' to an unusual sprawling habit; it will spread to at least twice its maximum height. On the edge of a terrace, or in a large pot, it will flow downwards, making a tremendous cascade of flowers. Plant it also at the front of a border where its trailing growth will intermingle decoratively with other low plants without overwhelming them; I have seen it looking marvellous sprawling between bushes of common lavender, *Lavandula angustifolia*, whose grey leaves and purple flowers accompany it especially well. It will flower well in a semi-shaded position.

Rosa 'Reine des Violettes'

Origin: France (Millet Malet) 1860
Height: 4ft/1.2m
Z: 5

This Hybrid Perpetual, with sumptuous flowers, will flower repeatedly throughout the season. From plump buds with decorative wing-like sepals, the colour at first shows crimson-red. The flowers open in June and are lavishly double, 3 1/2in/9cm across, a rich violet with pink and purple undertones. The petals, intricately veined in a deeper colour, are packed in tightly, swirling hither and yon, and arranged roughly in quarters. The flowers are lavishly blowsy just before they collapse, and their scent is deep, rich and musky. The foliage is boldly pinnate with shapely grey-green rounded and toothed leaflets. It forms an upright vigorous shrub with the flowers borne well aloft on almost thornless growth.

'Reine des Violettes' is outstanding among Hybrid Perpetuals and is especially to be recommended to gardeners who have not much room and want to enjoy the full old rose experience: lavish, beautifully formed flowers, marvellous scent, distinguished foliage and, in this case, recurrent-flowering. It would be excellent as the dominant plant in a modest mixed border; its colouring mixing equally well with a pink and blue colour scheme or with one in which vibrant reds and purples play their part. To give of its best, it does however need a sunny position.

Rosa 'Reine Victoria'

Origin: France (Schwartz) 1872
Height: 6ft/1.8m
Z: 5

Also known as 'La Reine Victoria', this Bourbon has memorably beautiful double, very cupped flowers with inward-curving petals, 2 1/2in/6cm across. They appear in June, borne in generous bunches, opening from plump green-and-red-striped buds, and are a soft salmon-pink of exactly the kind seen in old paintings, with a deeper colour within the flower. 'Reine Victoria' will flower recurrently after the first lavish blossoming, and the scent is light but emphatically sweet. It has very thorny new shoots and the leaves are decoratively toothed. It is famously susceptible to black spot.

The delicately cupped flowers, carried high at the tips of slender stems, give the whole bush an air of elegance and distinction. In the mixed border 'Reine Victoria' looks beautiful with herbaceous planting to echo the light silvery quality of its flowers. *Geranium* 'Johnson's Blue' and the refined lilac-pink spires of *Campanula latiloba* 'Hidcote Amethyst' both set off the colour very well. Later in the season it will associate well with the blue flowers and grey, finely cut foliage of *Caryopteris* × *clandonensis*. Avoid associating it with plants that have flowers that are too big and beefy. In habit it makes a rather upright bush, and in the border can have valuable structural presence.

Rosa 'René d'Anjou'

Origin: France (Robert)
1853
Height: 4ft/1.2m
Z: 5

This small Moss rose has exceptionally beautiful flowers and is decorative in all its detail. The buds are covered in moss, and open a lovely rosy pink. The flowers in June are double, 3in/8cm across, an exquisite pale pink with a touch of lilac. They are slightly cupped at first, the inner petals grouped in quarters and the outer petals curving backwards most gracefully, and have a light and spicy scent. As the flowers age they take on a more definite tone of mauve. The foliage is a healthy sparkling pale green, with new leaflets an attractive bronze colour and creased down the middle. New growth is covered in fine hairy thorns.

The exceptional flowers – in the first rank for beauty – are the greatest attraction of 'René d'Anjou'. It will flower in the semi-shade where its warm unfaded colour will be seen at its very best. In a small-scale mixed border it could be the most substantial shrub. Flowers with mauve in their colouring associate with it particularly well. The perennial wallflower, *Erysimum* 'Bowles' Mauve', with its added attractions of a very long flowering season and fine grey foliage, makes a marvellous partner. Or grow it accompanied by smaller herbaceous plants such as geraniums, pinks and violas which also provide sympathetic colours.

Rosa 'Robert le Diable'

Origin: France date unknown
Height: 4ft/1.2m
Z: 5

It is one of the oddities of garden plants that there are remarkably few really good reds in roses, old or new. This small Centifolia, an old rose of unknown date, is one of the best. Almost black-red globular buds open in June to beautiful loosely double flowers, 2in/5cm across, a brilliant crimson-red in colour and with a slight but sweet perfume. The petals have a sumptuous texture of velvet and the tips curve ouwards, making a most graceful shape. The centre of the flower has a green eye and the petals here have occasional shadowy stripes of pink. As the flowers fade the neat shape becomes more informal and the colour fades to a lilac-purple. The leathery leaves are edged in red and are slightly toothed.

'Robert le Diable' forms a neat bush with the dazzling red flowers held well above the foliage. It will certainly make a brilliant contribution to a bold scheme of reds and purples, in which purple foliage will show off the colour of the flowers to marvellous effect. It is a small bush, and low-growing herbaceous plants can be used to provide harmonious companions: for example, the profuse purple-brown foliage of *Euphorbia dulcis* 'Chameleon' surrounding its base is extremely effective, setting off its colour well.

Rosa 'Roseraie de l'Haÿ'

Origin: France
(Cochet-Cochet) 1901
Height: 6ft/1.8m
Z: 4

This immensely popular rose, often planted as a hedge along European motorways, is nevertheless an admirable garden plant. Its buds are long and shapely, with pointed sepals extending far beyond the tips. The flowers in early June are semi-double, 5in/13cm across, an excellent rich purple, and with a warm rich perfume. The petals have slightly ragged edges and a mind of their own, so that the flower always has an attractively dishevelled appearance, full of character. Flowers are produced throughout the season and the foliage is splendid, a fresh mid green with deeply veined gleaming leaves which in autumn take on a marvellous buttery colour. The hips are very striking – large, curvaceous, and orange in colour. It makes an upright bush of great presence.

It is a tribute to 'Roseraie de l'Haÿ' that, despite its ubiquity, it has preserved its charm. In the garden the rich colouring of its flowers makes it a superb plant for a border of purples and reds; its perpetual-flowering, shining foliage and shapely habit are additional qualities. I have seen it looking marvellous with the vibrant, deep violet-blue flowers of the herbaceous clematis *C. × durandii* growing through it. It flowers well in partial shade and is excellent for town gardens.

Rosa 'Salet'

Origin: France (Lacharme) 1854
Height: 4ft/1.2m
Z: 5

This delightful Moss rose has pink flowers of tremendous character. Its buds are very handsome: frilled, with whiskery sepals which as they open show bright red. The flowers in June are double, 3in/8cm across, a striking sugar-pink. The petals are loosely held in a roughly quartered pattern, reflexing backwards at the tips. The flowers are slightly cupped at first but as they age they assume a much more voluptuous, abandoned aspect. They have an exceptionally good sweet scent. The foliage is of a pretty light green with elegant floppy leaflets, slightly toothed. Flowers are held in generous clusters at the tips of upright stems which bristle with very fine hairy thorns.

'Salet' makes an upright shapely bush on which it displays its flowers throughout the season. It is one of the finest of the Mosses for the smaller garden. The warm pink of the flowers will associate happily with the blues and violets of campanulas, geraniums and lavender in high summer; in August and September it looks marvellous with the swaying sky-blue flowers of *Salvia uliginosa* rising above it. Use it also as an admirable pot plant: I have seen a pair looking beautiful flanking steps down into a sunny terrace, making an ornamental and deliciously scented entrance.

Rosa 'Scharlachglut'

Origin: Germany (Kordes) 1952
Height: 10ft/3m
Z: 5

This great modern shrub rose, also known as 'Scarlet Fire', is of Gallica parentage and seems to me to be the ideal type of new rose, combining character, exuberance and wildness. Its buds are elegant blood-red cones fringed with pointed sepals and opening in June into single flowers, 3 1/2in/9cm across with a rich sweet scent. The colour is true scarlet and the petals are the texture of the finest silk velvet, slightly frilly at the edges, and undulating. They are veined in deeper red and at their centre the stamens are rich gold. The leaves are very bold, rounded, pointed and toothed. The new growth is red in colour, thorny and very vigorous. It forms a very large open shrub with immense arching stems.

I can still remember first seeing this rose in the great garden at Kiftsgate Court. I was there late one afternoon when the low sunlight caught the flowers, making them glow in their partly-shaded site. It is admirable in a wild setting where its most striking colour gives it dramatic presence. In a border on the grandest scale, with a dramatic red colour scheme, it would be superlative in a central position. Although it flowers only once, it has a long season, and the bold foliage and decorative red hips in late summer prolong the interest. In any event, in a few weeks' of flowering, 'Scarlachglut' gives more excitement than many roses do in their whole lifetime.

Rosa 'Schneezwerg'

Origin: Germany (Lambert) 1912
Height: 5ft/1.5m
Z: 4

This hybrid between *R. rugosa* and an unknown rose is one of the most valuable of the medium-sized shrub roses. It starts to flower in June, when pointed creamy pink buds open into 2 1/2in/6cm semi-double white flowers. Petals with slightly frilly edges reveal a striking bush of stamens at the centre, and the beautiful glistening pinnate foliage with fern-like leaves make a marvellous background to the flowers. These have only a slight scent. Hips in characteristic Rugosa fashion, round and plump like little apples, are produced at the same time as the flowers; later in the season they mature into very decorative orange-red fruits.

'Schneezwerg' forms a shapely vigorous bush and, with its very decorative foliage and procession of beautiful flowers, is one of the best repeat-flowering white roses, flowering well in the partial shade. In a cool pale colour scheme, with whites, creams and yellows, it is a most valuable ingredient. *Lychnis coronaria* 'Alba', with white flowers and silver foliage, and yellow perpetual-flowering *Anthemis tinctoria* 'E.C. Buxton' make admirable partners. 'Schneezwerg' is also admirable for structural planting, and can even be clipped as a hedge. Or place a pair on either side of a gate or door, preferably in the semi-shade that displays its gleaming foliage and pale flowers so well.

Rosa 'Soupert et Notting'

Origin: France (Pernet)
1874
Height: 36in/90cm
Z: 5

The more compact Moss roses are valuable plants in the smaller garden, often possessing, in reduced form but in proportion, all the beauty of the larger shrub roses. The curiously named 'Soupert et Notting' is a good example. It has splendid buds enclosed in mossy sepals which part to show the rich red of the swelling bud. The striking flowers appear in June, at first delicately cupped but later opening into double, rich pink blooms, 2 1/2in/6cm across, with a delicious, intense perfume. A second flowering occurs in the late summer. The flowers are slightly irregular and the packed petals swirl in different directions, giving a lively appearance. The foliage is a good pale green in colour, and the new growth bristles with countless fine red thorns.

'Soupert et Notting' flowers profusely and produces a useful second flowering. It has very striking flowers of a lively colour and an excellent scent. It is small enough to fit into any garden, and yet it has all the presence of something much larger. It is a good plant in a border but it is also very suitable for planting in a pot, when it must be fed and watered copiously. It forms a neat, densely leafed bush which may be clipped in winter to keep it shapely. I have seen it splendidly used in a little box-edged parterre in a town garden.

Rosa 'Stanwell Perpetual'

Origin: England (Lee and Kennedy) 1838
Height: 5ft/1.5m
Z: 4

This beautiful rose was a natural seedling of the Northern European native, *R. pimpinellifolia*, the Scotch or Burnet Rose. From these wild origins it inherits its splendidly healthy character. The flowers are quite different from those seen in the wild, opening from neat little buds into lovely double flowers 1 1/2in/4cm across, at first a clear shell-pink but becoming almost white with age, with a sweet spicy scent. At first they are cupped but as they age they open out flat with backward-curving petals. After the first flowering in June it produces further blossoms throughout the season. The delicate little grey-green leaves and many thorned stems are typical of the Scotch Rose. Some of the leaves turn reddish-brown but this is not a disease and is no cause for alarm. New growth, pale pistachio-green, is armed with fine red thorns.

For its perpetual flowering, its air of distinction and its graceful new growth, 'Stanwell Perpetual' is outstanding among the smaller shrub roses. It is an excellent ingredient in a mixed border, particularly one of modest size. In colour it consorts easily with many other plants, but be careful to choose those that will not be outshone by its delicacy and distinction. I have seen it looking very beautiful in late summer among white Japanese anemones, *A. × hybrida* 'Honorine Jobert', and it would look equally good with the type, which is a warm pink.

Rosa stellata mirifica

Origin: South west USA
Height: 5ft/1.5m
Z: 6

The wild roses, apart from their natural beauty, frequently make very tough, disease-resistant garden plants. This splendid shrub, known as the 'Sacramento Rose', is a good example. Its pointed buds open in June into dazzling single flowers, 2in/5cm across, a fresh cerise-pink, only lightly scented. Undulating petals, silky in texture and delicately etched with veins of a darker colour, overlap slightly, making a graceful shape. The centre of the flowers is strikingly ornamented with a prominent tuft of stamens. The foliage is decorative, with very small toothed grey-green leaves resembling those of a gooseberry, and the stems boldly armed with countless very long pale thorns. A profusion of plump little red hips is produced in late summer.

As species roses go, *R. stellata mirifica* makes a dense and shapely bush. Its unsophisticated but striking flowers, of a lovely colour and distinguished character, would make a lively contribution to the border. Although it flowers once only, the beautiful foliage gives long-lasting pleasure. It will add a sharp, sprightly note among reds and purples, and I have seen it looking marvellous alongside a bush of the plum-coloured *Berberis thunbergii atropurpurea*, making a fine contrast of flower and foliage. To flower really well it must have a sunny position.

Rosa 'Surpasse Tout'

Origin: France before 1832
Height: 4ft/1.2m
Z: 4

This sumptuous Gallica has cheerful cerise-red flowers, an unusual colour in the group. It has beautiful plump buds with intricate pointed sepals which part to show a deep red. The flowers in June are double, very large, 4 1/2in/11cm across, a vivid red-pink. The petals in the centre, occasionally splashed with silver-pink, twist and turn, while those round the edge overlap in vaguely concentric circles. The flowers are lightly but sweetly scented, and handsomely held in generous clusters on tall stems that bristle with fine hair-like thorns. The foliage is pale green with curved, toothed leaves.

'Surpasse Tout', with its showy but distinguished flowers and good foliage, will overpower anything weak and insipid beside it. It needs to be part of a dramatic and lively scheme, and will make a brilliant contribution to a boldly colourful arrangement of pinks, reds and purples in a mixed border. It looks splendid accompanied by the much deeper maroon of *Knautia macedonica*, whose flowers sway airily aloft on tall stems and, against a background of clouds of the bronze-purple leaves of the fennel *Foeniculum vulgare* 'Purpureum'. Silver foliage, too, is a magnificent partner for its lively colour: the big wormwood *Artemisia absinthium* 'Lambrook Silver' is especially

good – but remove the stems of its dull yellow flowers before they open. 'Surpasse Tout' has a tendency, like other Gallicas, to become a little leggy; it helps to prune weak shoots after flowering, to encourage stronger growth from the base.

Rosa 'The Countryman'

Origin: Britain (Austin) 1987
Height: 36in/90cm
Z: 5

This recently introduced variety is the offspring of an old Portland rose and a modern garden cultivar. From prettily tufted buds the flowers open in June, at first cupped and globe-shaped, and shell-pink. When fully open they are double, 3 1/2in/9cm across, with a lively pattern of swirling petals whose tips are silver-pink in contrast to the deeper pink at the base, giving it something of the appearance of a dahlia. The flowers are carried in immense profusion and their perfume is excellent – deep, spicy and sweet. There is a second flowering later in the season, and there may be scattered flowers in between. The foliage is light green with slightly toothed leaflets.

'The Countryman' is a little short in stature for the size and profusion of its flowers, but is an admirable

Illustration opposite:
Rosa 'The Countryman'

candidate for a small mixed border where its defect will be concealed in a tapestry of colour. Its warm pink looks beautiful with the rich blue of the perennial flax, *Linum perenne*, or with the silver-blue of *Geranium* 'Johnson's Blue' whose long flowering shoots will scramble through the shrub. It also looks very beautiful planted with *Caryopteris* × *clandonensis*, of similar height to the rose, with grey foliage and clouds of lively blue flowers in late summer. Or plant it in a pot with a ruff of *Helichrysum petiolare* about its legs.

Rosa 'Tricolore de Flandre'

Origin: Belgium (Van Houtte) 1846
Height: 36in/90cm
Z: 4

This little Gallica is particularly valuable for the smaller garden. Fat scarlet and white buds, on the tips of upright stems, open in June into double flowers 2 1/2in/6cm across, cupped very neatly at first but opening out fully, striped in pink and purple and becoming more purple as they age. They have an excellent, spicy scent. The flowers last for a long season, and their interest lies partly in the variation of colours and appearance during their various stages. The foliage is a good pale green with deeply veined leaflets.

This vigorous, compact rose, forming a bush as wide as it is high, will make an extremely ornamental contribution to a small-sized bed, among plants to scale. Its flowers are quite small and delicate, so that any associated planting should be chosen carefully to avoid swamping its fragile charms. It flowers only

once, and to maintain interest should be accompanied by more perpetual, or later-flowering herbaceous plants, such as diascias, penstemons, pinks or trailing violas (such as *V. cornuta*). I have seen it looking very well with an underplanting of the pale pink-flowered *Geranium endressii* 'Wargrave's Pink'.

Rosa 'Tuscany Superb'

Origin: Garden before 1848
Height: 4ft/1.2m
Z: 4

Sometimes known as the 'Old Velvet Rose', this Gallica has marvellous character. Its origins are rather vague but it is thought to be very much older than its first recorded date. Very pointed buds with long twisting sepals open in June to form bold, flat, semi-double flowers, 3 1/2in/9cm across. They are a rich velvet-maroon in colour, with striking golden stamens, and the crimped petals curl and overlap, causing variations in colour from red-maroon to almost black-purple, creating a sumptuous effect. They have a spicy perfume, not powerful but emphatic. 'Tuscany Superb' has particularly handsome pale green pinnate foliage with curving and creased leaflets, and new growth bristles with very fine hairy thorns. The rose 'Tuscany' is almost identical but has rather smaller flowers with fewer petals.

'Tuscany Superb' makes a vigorous upright bush and, with its dramatic flowers well set off by fresh green foliage, it forms a spectacular ornamental plant. It makes an admirable ingredient in bold plantings of red and purple, and is wonderful planted in front of much larger shrubs with purple foliage, such as *Cotinus coggygria* 'Royal Purple' or the purple-leafed filbert, *Corylus maxima* 'Purpurea'. The much smaller *Berberis* 'Atropurpurea Nana', with its diminutive plum-coloured leaves, makes an excellent associated shrub, rising to just below the height of the rose.

Rosa 'Variegata di Bologna'

Origin: Italy (Bonfiglioli) 1903
Height: 5ft/1.5m
Z: 5

'Variegata di Bologna', a Bourbon of surprisingly recent introduction, has a splendidly cheerful air, with flowers smudged and striped in crimson. Its plump buds are especially pretty, showing stripes of red against white, and framed in pointed sepals. The flowers open in June, cupped, very double pale pink, 3in/8cm across, dashingly striped with deep crimson-purple, like some precious piece of old enamelled jewellery. At first they are very neatly formed: cupped, with swirling petals in the centre and a crisply defined outer ring. Later they become wonderfully full and blowsy. They are lightly scented and show up well against the background of grey-green leaves. There is the occasional scattering of flowers later in the season.

This striking rose makes an excellent decorative punctuation mark in a mixed border. Its rather lax growth means that it usually needs support, and it may be trained very effectively on a tripod. It is susceptible to mildew. The flowers are so striking that associated planting should be quiet and simple: pinks, greys, violet-blues and the occasional sprightly note of purple-red are the colours that will work best. Emphatic clumps of the catmint *Nepeta* 'Six Hills Giant' look splendid with it.

Illustration: *Rosa* 'Wolley-Dod'

Rosa villosa

Origin: Northern Europe
Height: 5ft/1.5m
Z: 5

The Apple Rose is a northern European native. It forms a suckering bush with very handsome grey-green foliage and single pink flowers that are followed by beautiful elongated scarlet hips. The foliage has boldly rounded leaflets with a sweet apple scent. I have grown this rose in the orchard where, in a wild sort of way, it was very decorative. Far more ornamental and garden-worthy, is the double-flowered form, *R. v.* 'Duplex', or *R.* 'Wolley-Dod'. Hairy buds, with very fine and intricate sepals, open in June to clear, warm pink semi-double flowers, 3in/8cm across, with curling, overlapping petals and striking stamens. It will produce further flowers later in the season, which suggests that it is most likely to be a hybrid rather than a true form.

With its pink flowers against distinguished grey-green foliage, 'Wolley-Dod' is a most ornamental plant. The type is best in an informal, but not necessarily wild, setting. But 'Wolley-Dod' is more versatile. I have seen it very successfully grown, fringed with bushes of lavender in an ornamental kitchen garden. But it also makes an excellent shrub for the border where its decorative flowers, superb foliage and particularly ornamental hips will have a telling effect over a very long period.

Rosa 'White Pet'

Origin: USA (Henderson) 1879
Height: 24in/60cm
Z: 5

Formerly known as 'Little White Pet', this arose as a sport of the Rambler 'Félicité Perpétue'. It is all too easy to think of it as the horticultural equivalent of wallpaper but, in spite of its undoubted versatility, it is in fact a plant of some character. Starting in June it produces from decorative red-pink buds an endless profusion of neat white rosettes, 1 1/2in/4cm across. The flowers pass through four distinct stages: tight pink buds, half-open cupped flower with red and pink outer petals, neatly formed rosette (still with the occasional flush of pink), and finally a more loosely formed double, almost pure white flower. The foliage is very handsome: dark green, very healthy in appearance with neatly shaped leaflets, toothed and pointed. It is extremely tough and will flower in almost any position.

Few roses are as perpetual-flowering as 'White Pet'. In very small gardens it is a marvellous ingredient in a little mixed border. By putting it with other miniature plants such as diascias, pinks, the smaller geraniums and violas, the effect of a much bigger border can be reproduced. It is also an excellent pot plant: a pair flanking a little path or gateway make admirable ornaments, and it is also very effective in a mixed planting in a container.

Rosa 'William Lobb'

Origin: France (Laffay)
1855
Height: 7ft/2m
Z: 5

This Moss rose, formerly known as 'Old Velvet Moss' and 'Duchesse d'Istrie', is a substantial shrub with strikingly beautiful deep purple flowers. Its stems and buds are well mossed and the buds are fringed with pointed sepals. The flowers in June are double, 3in/8cm across, a marvellous rich crimson-purple, with the colour and texture of the exotic velvets of the past. The flowers are slightly cupped at first, with twisting and curved petals giving an animated texture. As the flowers age they become looser and the colour fades to a deep dusty lilac. They have a heady sweet scent and are carried high aloft in bold clusters. The foliage is handsome, with shapely toothed and rounded leaves with a leathery surface.

This is an aristocratic rose – in flower colour, in its vigorous, upright growth and in its striking, leathery foliage. It has great presence at the back of a mixed border, but related plantings need to be carefully judged. It has a tendency to become leggy, a defect that may be concealed with lower planting in front. I have seen it used successfully in a purple and red border with lavender and *Berberis* 'Atropurpurea Nana' at the front, and framed by clouds of feathery purple fennel, *Foeniculum vulgare* 'Purpureum'.

Rosa 'Winchester Cathedral'

Origin: Britain (Austin) 1988
Height: 4ft/1.2m
Z: 5

This recently introduced modern shrub rose has outstanding qualities. Pale pink buds open in June into double white flowers, 4in/10cm across, with an excellent, sweet scent. The shape of the flowers is at first crisply defined but as they age they become more loose and the petals, with scalloped edges that twist and curl, create a lively, informal appearance. At the centre the flowers are suffused with cream, and there are occasional little splashes of pink on the petals. The flowers are carried high, in clusters at the tips of stems. After the June flowering they continue to appear throughout the season. The foliage is dark green with toothed leaves. Flowers are produced repeatedly throughout the season.

'Winchester Cathedral' forms a neat shapely shrub and its lavish well perfumed flowers are beautiful. The touch of cream that suffuses the flowers makes them particularly beautiful with creams and pinks, especially plants such as *Diascia rigescens* which combine the two colours. It looks beautiful, too, with softer creamy yellows such as that of *Sisyrinchium striatum* which, only a little lower in height, associates very well with it. This is one of the very best white roses for the smaller garden. Plant it in a pot where it makes a wonderful summer-long ornament.

Rosa xanthina hugonis

Origin: China
Height: 8ft/2.5m
Z: 5

This great wild rose, formerly known as *R. hugonis*, produces exquisite flowers early in the year, and forms a shrub of spectacular beauty. The buds are very striking: long and pointed with a marked spherical base which becomes the hip. The partly open flower grows upright, like a candle, showing its beautiful colour, a glowing primrose-yellow. The fully open flowers at the end of May are single, gently cupped, 2 1/2in/6cm across, with a mass of stamens of an identical yellow, and have a light sweet scent. The petals have slightly frilly edges, overlapping gracefully, and become a darker yellow towards the centre. The foliage is most beautiful: mid grey-green with very small toothed leaflets pleated down the centre. Leaves turn a fine tawny brown in autumn and there is a profusion of maroon hips. New growth is red-brown and well thorned.

A mature bush of *R. xanthina hugonis*, with its yellow flowers glowing against grey-green leaves, is one of the loveliest sights in the garden in late spring. Plant it in the wildest place you have, among trees and shrubs. It could form the centrepiece of a wonderful yellow spring garden, with other flowering shrubs such as *Corylopsis pauciflora*, bulbs such as narcissi or crown imperials, *Fritillaria imperialis* 'Maxima Lutea' and perhaps an underplanting of *Euphorbia polychroma* which produces burgeoning mounds of fresh yellow bracts.

Rosa 'Zigeunerknabe'

Origin: Germany
(Lambert) 1909
Height: 6ft/1.8m
Z: 5

This, also known as 'Gypsy Boy', a translation of its German name, is a modern shrub rose, sometimes classified as a Bourbon. The fat globe-shaped buds are fringed with pointed sepals which part to show a rich red, and the flowers, which open in June, are double, 2 1/2in/6cm across, deep crimson-purple, with striking golden-yellow stamens and an exotic, sweet scent. The petals are subtly marbled in a pale silver-purple, giving a shimmering effect, and as the flowers age the crimson fades to red-purple. The flowers are carried in clusters at the tips of slender upright stems, and the leaves are well rounded, toothed and of an attractive fresh green. Orange-red hips are produced in late summer.

'Zigeunerknabe' is a very tough rose that will tolerate poor conditions. Its bold presence could provide the major ingredient of a large-scale mixed border with a red and purple scheme. Its growth is rather lax and it will benefit from support – an ornamental tripod would display it well. Its crimson flowers look marvellous with big purple-leafed shrubs like cotinus or berberis.

CLIMBING
ROSES

❧

In this section I include roses which, whatever their natural inclination, are best grown trained on a wall, fence or other support. Some of the roses included in the previous section on 'Bush Roses', with long flexible shoots, may also be used as climbers in small gardens.

To many gardeners the sight of a great climbing rose in full flower, swathing an arbour or cascading from the branches of a tree, is one of the greatest of pleasures. There is no doubt of their beauty – but they also have a practical advantage. The amount of ground space occupied by them is very small and most of their growth will be in space that would otherwise be unusable. In smaller gardens this immensely increases possibilities. In gardens where there is not so much pressure on space, climbing roses may provide a marvellous dramatic backdrop to plantings in borders. They can also be used – on posts or tripods – to give vertical emphasis within a bed. Other plants, trees or larger shrubs, also make excellent supports for climbing roses, often providing decorative interest when the rose is not in flower.

The range of climbing roses is vast. They vary from the spectacular giants such as *Rosa filipes* 'Kiftsgate' to the small-sized 'Goldfinch' which could fit into almost any garden. In character and colour of flower they show tremendous variety – from the big white flowers of *Rosa laevigata*

'Cooperi' to the diminutive creamy pink rosettes of 'Adélaïde d'Orléans'. For almost any part of the garden, from the most formal to the least formal, there is an appropriate climbing rose that will give exactly the emphasis that is needed. In full flower in mid-summer, these climbing roses seem to be the very essence of ornamental gardening.

Rosa 'Adélaïde d'Orléans'

Origin: France (Jacques) 1826
Height: 15ft/4.5m
Z: 5

The vigorous growth of this old Rambler, and the delicacy of its flowers, make a marvellous contrast. Buds hang in profuse clusters, showing pink as the sepals part, and the flowers, opening in June, are semi-double 2in/5cm across, the colour of faded old lace, suffused here and there with pink. They are perfumed with a light sweet scent. The petals are slightly crumpled and irregular, the texture of very fine silk, and those at the centre form a little ruff about the golden stamens. The foliage is a distinguished dark green with elegant little leaves that usually remain evergreen.

In its early stages of flowering, with the beautifully neat creamy pink buds appearing at the same time as the rumpled but exquisite flowers, 'Adélaïde d'Orléans' makes a sumptuous and enchanting sight. Although it flowers only once, the beauty of the flowering is so splendid that one is happy to live with a rather unexciting plant for the rest of the year. It makes one of the very best roses for training on an arbour or pergola, where the slender and whippy flowering shoots can be allowed to cascade downwards. Here, other later-flowering plants such as clematis and vines may take over when the rose has finished flowering.

Rosa 'Aimée Vibert'

Origin: France (Vibert)
1828
Height: 12ft/3.6m
Z: 5

Also known under the charming name 'Bouquet de la Mariée', this Rambler is one of the oldest cultivars among all the climbing roses. Its buds are very ornamental – clusters of little globes showing rich pink as they start to open – and the partly opened flower is still flushed with pink. The flowers, opening rather late in June, are loosely double, 2in/5cm across, white but with a hint of creamy pink. They are beautifully formed, with the petals standing well up, forming a full rosette, and have a light sweet scent. The foliage is particularly striking, with boldly shaped rounded and pointed leaflets with a glistening surface.

This is one of the very best of the climbing roses. The lavish clusters of lovely flowers, intermingled with pink buds in different stages of opening, make a most striking spectacle. And unlike most Ramblers, 'Aimée Vibert' repeat flowers well, continuing deep into autumn. It is especially valuable for the smaller garden where, neatly trained over an arbour or forming the chief ingredient of a pergola, it will be decorative over a very long season.

Rosa 'Albéric Barbier'

Origin: France (Barbier)
1900
Height: 15ft/4.5m
Z: 5

In all respects this is one of the most beautiful of the Ramblers. Its exceptionally good foliage – healthy, rich green, with a gleaming surface – has the additional advantage of being almost evergreen. Shapely pale lemon-yellow buds open in June into white flowers with pale yellow centres, very double, 3in/8cm across, and with the appearance of crushed material. After the first profuse flowering there will be scattered flowers throughout the season, and the flowers are perfumed with a delicious sweet scent. New growth has a striking ruddy colour with bold red thorns. As it flowers on the previous year's growth, any pruning should be done soon after flowering.

At its peak, with its beautiful mixture of yellow opening buds, off-white flowers and sparkling foliage, 'Albéric Barbier' is marvellously decorative. It will enliven any corner of the garden, especially a partly shaded one where it will be seen to especially good effect. It is a good rose for a well planned arbour where its beautiful leaves and occasional flowers will make lively ornament throughout the season. Trained on a wall or fence at the back of a border its foliage makes an excellent backdrop to other plantings.

Rosa 'Albertine'

Origin: France (Barbier)
1912
Height: 15ft/4.5m
Z: 5

Of all the Ramblers 'Albertine' is one of the most popular – and deservedly so, if only for its scent. This – intensely sweet and deep – is among the finest of any rose; on a hot summer's evening it will waft great distances, pervading the garden. 'Albertine' has striking, glistening foliage flushed with red when young. The flower buds are red at first but become a distinctive rich apricot-pink opening into neatly scrolled half-open buds. The flowers, which open fully in June, are generous, pink and double, 3 1/2in/9cm

across. Some of the petals at the edge curl backwards at the tips, while those in the middle make a swirling pattern. As the flowers age they become increasingly loose and blowsy, like a gently crushed silk handkerchief, paling almost to white. The new growth is flushed with red.

For its fabulous scent alone 'Albertine' is worth a place in the garden. It is a bold, brassy and very vigorous rose, not one for the delicate effect. It forms well-thorned stout branches, and although its lower branches can look rather coarse and ungainly, if used on a wall or fence at the back of a border, other plants can conceal that defect. It is said to be less prone to mildew if trained on a pergola or arbour. I have seen the deep purple clematis 'Etoile Violette' climbing 'Albertine's' lower limbs to make a dazzling colour combination.

Rosa 'Alister Stella Gray'

Origin: Britain (Grey) 1894
Height: 15ft/4.5m
Z: 5

Floriferous abundance, fabulous scent and delicacy are the combined virtues of this climbing Noisette which is also known as 'Golden Rambler'. Elegant yellow buds open in June to form creamy white double flowers, 3in/8cm across. The flowers are beautifully formed of petals that curl and fold, with a fine silky texture. They are borne in great profusion, giving off a marvellous tropical fruit scent of exceptional intensity, and will continue throughout the season, even into October. Good fresh green foliage is very decorative with finely toothed and pointed leaflets.

Trained round a gate, or over a porch leading into the house, 'Alister Stella Gray' will provide a delicious scented entrance as well as presenting close-up views of its flowers. It flowers well in partial shade where its flowers will fade much less quickly than in full sun. It may also be grown satisfactorily as a shrub; in a border it will form a fountain of flowers, marvellous as the centrepoint in a scheme of creams and yellows, with, for example, the equally perpetual-flowering *Anthemis tinctoria* 'E.C.Buxton', the pale yellow perennial foxglove, *Digitalis grandiflora*, and golden-yellow daylilies later in the season.

Rosa banksiae var. *banksiae*

Origin: China 1807
Height: 25ft/7.5m
Z: 7

The white double-flowered Banksian rose, not so frequently seen as its yellow sister described below, is a marvellous though tender climber. It is evergreen, thornless, and the new growth of both shoots and leaves is tinged with red. Clusters of little flowers appear in late April or May, very double with frilled tips to the petals, 1 1/2in/3cm across. Their colour is a creamy off-white and the scent, intensely sweet with a hint of violets, is one of the most beautiful. Like many of the wild roses it is healthy and vigorous; indeed its vigour may be its only drawback, especially in a small garden, and it should be ruthlessly pruned. It may be cut back at almost any time, but remember that it flowers only on the previous year's growth. I have cut it hard back even as late as August and it has flowered well the following year.

In gardens fortunate enough to provide the climate that suits it, the white Banksian rose will give one of the most beautiful displays of any late spring-flowering plant. The creamy white of the flowers and the simple elegance of the foliage make it an admirable partner for other climbing or wall plants; it looks beautiful with early-flowering ceanothus. Except in the very mildest places it will need the protection of a sunny wall to flower well; a pergola or arbour would not provide the shelter it needs.

Rosa banksiae 'Lutea'

Origin: China c.1825
Height: 25ft/7.5m
Z: 7

In growth the yellow Banksian rose closely resembles *R. banksiae* var. *banksiae*, but the flowers are a very delicate yellow, slightly smaller, 1in/2.5cm across and without scent. Some authorities claim that it is slightly scented but I have sniffed countless examples and never detected any perfume.

In a sunny place it will flower prolifically, with cascades of blossom, providing one of the most dazzling sights of any spring-flowering climber. The softness of the yellow harmonises excellently with other climbing plants appearing in the same season, such as the rich blue of *Clematis alpina* 'Frances Rivis'. Like *R. b.* var. *banksiae* it may prove too vigorous for comfort, and should be vigorously pruned back.

Rosa 'Blairii Number Two'

Origin: Britain (Blair)
1845
Height: 12ft/3.6m
Z: 5

This rather absurdly named rose is a distinguished old climbing Bourbon with much to recommend it. From very fat buds double flowers open in June, 3 1/2in/9cm across, a lovely warm pink at the centre but fading to silver-pink at the tips of the petals and at the edge of the flower. This variation in colour is what strikes the eye. The perfume is sweet and fresh. Leaves are bold and shapely, and new growth is an attractive red-brown. It sometimes produces a second scattering of flowers at the end of the season. 'Blairii Number One', rarely seen, is identical in all respects except that it is paler in colour and flowers less generously. However, its flowers, especially at the height of their development, are very beautiful, with outer petals curving crisply backwards and the frilly edges to petals giving a delightfully romantic appearance.

The profuse flowering of distinctly glamorous, well-scented flowers is the chief attraction of 'Blairi Number Two'. It will flower well in the semi-shade where its soft colour will last better than in the full sun. It looks wonderful on a pergola, where its delicious scent is near at hand and its heavy flowers well displayed above eye-level.

Rosa 'Bleu Magenta'

Origin: France c.1900
Height: 15ft/4.5m
Z: 5

The colour of this Rambler is very unusual. The flowers, starting late in June and continuing for a very long season, form profuse clusters of double rosettes 2in/5cm across, a marvellous deep purple-red fading to a dark bruised lilac, with glimpses of bright yellow stamens. The petals overlap and curl, giving each flower a lively appearance. They are marvellously scented. The foliage is a very healthy pale green with a shining surface, and leaflets are strikingly toothed.

'Bleu Magenta' will flower well in partial shade where its deep purple will last much longer before fading. On a pergola or trained over an arbour, it is especially beautiful, with the light shining through the pale green foliage and illuminating the hanging purple flowers. Trained on a wall or fence 'Bleu Magenta' makes an admirable backdrop to a border of rich reds and purples, and looks marvellous with any plant with purple or copper foliage: the ornamental grape vine *Vitis vinifera* 'Purpurea', with dusty purple leaves, provides a brilliant partner, continuing to be decorative in both foliage and fruit long after the rose has stopped flowering. Or plant it with a summer-flowering clematis such as 'Ernest Markham', whose magenta-red flowers, will overlap with those of the rose.

Rosa 'Blush Noisette'

Origin: USA (Noisette) before 1817
Height: 10ft/3m
Z: 5

This old cultivar, also known as 'Noisette Carnée', is one of the oldest surviving American varieties of rose. It is, properly speaking, a bush, but produces long lax growth that is far more satisfactory grown as a climber. It starts to flower in June, when numerous little rosy purple buds clustered at the tips of growth open first into elegant cupped flowers and eventually into semi-double flowers, 2in/5cm across, with a delicate spicy scent. The petals twist and overlap and are a very attractive lilac-pink. Leaves are pale green and new growth is almost thornless.

This is a most decorative and valuable rose. Not only does it flower very freely, but it will produce its sweetly scented flowers throughout the season. It has a reputation for lack of hardiness but I have grown it in a rather cold garden against an east-facing shady wall, where it flourished and gave much pleasure, being visible from the kitchen sink. Its exceptionally long flowering season, ornamental colouring and delicious scent make it a particularly good rose for the smaller garden in which major plants must earn their keep. Train it on a wall or fence at the back of a modest border, or use it trained round a tall tripod or framework obelisk as a splendid eye-catcher in the centre of a larger one. The sympathetic pale pink-purple of the flowers harmonises with both pale blues and pinks, as well as with richer purples and reds.

Rosa 'Blush Rambler'

Origin: Britain (Cant) 1903
Height: 15ft/4.5m
Z: 5

This is the ideal cottage garden Rambler: it is vigorous, floriferous, richly perfumed, artless but full of irresistible charm. Beautiful deep pink buds, shaped like rounded cones, with striking star-shaped sepals, open in June to an immense profusion of flowers carried in lavish trusses. Soft pink and white apple-blossom flowers are semi-double, 1 1/2in/4cm across, coloured in soft pink and white, with slightly curling petals and a prominent tuft of stamens at the centre. The perfume is rich and sweet. The foliage is pale green with elegantly veined leaflets.

This marvellous Rambler is too prolific of foliage and flower to mix easily with other plants, but it is lovely used alone on a simple pergola where, being almost thornless, it will not scratch passers-by. On an arbour or wall its marvellous profusion of flowers, falling in great cascades, will be displayed at their best. Or train it up a big fruit-tree in the orchard where the unsophisticated beauty of its flowers will have the perfect setting.

Rosa 'Bobbie James'

Origin: Britain
(Sunningdale) 1960
Height: 25ft/7.5m
Z: 5

This lovely Rambler was the discovery of Graham Stuart Thomas when he worked at Sunningdale Nurseries. Little whiskery buds, carried in giant clusters, show at first a lively red, changing to pink and finally opening in June into creamy white, slightly double flowers, 2in/5cm across. The petals are rounded and notched at the tips, and vary in number from flower to flower – some of which are single. They have very striking egg-yolk-yellow stamens and a delicious rich scent. The foliage is beautiful: a gleaming pale green with very large pointed and curved leaflets, up to 4in/10cm long. Flowers are carried on reddish-brown new growth.

'Bobbie James' is exceptional for its vigour, its marvellously decorative foliage and its beautiful and prolific richly perfumed flowers. Although wild and vigorous in its nature, its flowers are very delicate. It is very thorny and will climb readily through trees or anything else into which it may be allowed to grow. It is at its very best in a naturalistic setting; certainly it is no plant for artfully contrived schemes. Anyone who has seen it festooning the limbs of a tree with cascades of flowers will not easily forget the sight.

Rosa bracteata

Origin: South east China (1793)
Height: 20ft/6m
Z: 7

The Macartney Rose, named after the man who introduced it to the West, needs a warm and sunny garden and a lot of room. Any gardener who can meet those needs should grow it – it is one of the most beautiful of all wild roses. From neat pointed buds the flowers open in late May. They are single, white, 3 1/2in/9cm across, with a bush of pale lemon-yellow stamens at the centre. They have a pure sweet scent. The petals are fine in texture, and slightly frilled and crimped at the tips. After the first flowering it will produce flowers intermittently deep into the autumn, and large orange-red hips from late summer. Evergreen foliage has grey-green finely toothed leaflets. It has a rather twiggy dense growth and flowers are carried on short stems, nestling among the leaves.

The Macartney Rose, although wild and natural in character, looks very well at the back of the mixed border – provided there is space – where its evergreen foliage and dense growth make an excellent background to other plants. Its lovely delicate flowers, produced over a very long period, will associate happily with countless other plants; but there is always the risk that its subtle charms may be hidden. *R. bracteata* will almost certainly need the protection of a wall, although it is said to flower well on a north wall in warm places.

Rosa brunonii

Origin: Himalayas
Height: 40ft/12m
Z: 7

Anyone with enough room and the right climate should certainly grow this immense and immensely beautiful Rambler. Perhaps no other rose combines such vigour with such beauty of foliage and flower. The foliage is a lovely glaucous-grey with elegant long pointed drooping leaflets up 4in/10cm long. Shapely buds, becoming long and pointed and creamy yellow just before flowering, open rather late in June or early July, revealing single white flowers, up to 2in/5cm across. The petals at first overlap slightly but when the flower matures they separate completely. The stamens are especially striking: golden-yellow and profuse, becoming almost black at the tips with age. The scent of the flowers is vibrantly sweet. Flowers are borne in generous clusters, and new growth is spectacular with big red backward-pointing thorns. A cultivar, *R. b.* 'La Mortola', named after the great garden on the Italian Riviera, is even more vigorous and more prolific in flower, and individual flowers are larger, up to 3in/8cm across, and have distinctive little points to the tips of the petals.

Majestic is not a word to use too often for a rose, but *R. brunonii*, and especially 'La Mortola', deserves it. It is a plant for the wildest part of the garden – in the garden at La Mortola it cascades through trees on the edge of a rocky ravine. I grew it, perhaps a little tamely, through hawthorn and hazelnuts in an old field hedge. In most gardens it would be best planted to climb a substantial tree, where it will need cosseting at first in what is almost certain to be dry shade. When it has grown big enough to reach the lower branches of the tree its thorns will enable it to scramble through and support itself. Despite its reputation for tenderness, it survived in my garden a temperature of −17°F.

Rosa 'Céline Forestier'

Origin: France (Trouillard) 1842
Height: 12ft/3.6m
Z: 5

'Céline Forestier', a Noisette, is one of the most valuable of the smaller climbing roses. The shapely little leaves are pale green and flutter elegantly; the stems are flushed with red and heavily barbed. The buds, striped red and green, open into very double pale creamy yellow flowers, a richer golden-yellow towards the centre, 3in/8cm across, and with the appearance of crushed silk. They are fabulously scented – rich, sweet and with spicy undertones. The flowers, borne in clusters, start in May but will continue to appear intermittently throughout the summer.

This is one of the very best of the yellow-flowered roses, with plenty of character and an exceptional scent. The tips of shoots are prone to die back, although in general this is an admirably healthy rose. Because of its relatively modest size and gentle growth, 'Céline Forestier' is the perfect climbing rose for the small garden, where its repeat-flowering will be especially valued. I grow it trained against an old stone wall where it intermingles decoratively with plants in the

border below: *Elaeagnus* 'Quicksilver' with its silver grey foliage, and the white-flowered sweet rocket, *Hesperis matronalis* 'Alba', with whose intense peppery perfume it makes a memorable cocktail. In a border with pale colours, say creams and blues, 'Céline Forestier', would be magnificent as a centrepiece, trained on a column or tripod.

Rosa 'City of York'

Origin: Germany (Tantau) 1945
Height: 15ft/4.5m
Z: 5

There are very few modern climbing or rambling roses that are excellent in all respects: in flower, scent, foliage and general character. This splendid Rambler, also known as 'Direktor Benschop', is one. Its shapely buds have pointed tips and decorative sepals, and as they swell they reveal a pink-cream within. The flowers in June are at first cupped but open out semi-double, 3 1/2in/9cm across, creamy white with a pale yellow centre and profuse stamens. The petals are well rounded at their tips, and some curl decoratively inwards. The flowers are superbly scented – a rich sweet perfume – and the foliage is marvellous, with shining, dark green, slightly toothed leaflets.

Although bursting with health and vigour, this beautiful rose has no trace of coarseness. Like all white roses whose whiteness is softened by another colour, it is particularly valuable in the garden where, trained on a wall, fence or substantial tripod, in a white or predominantly pale-coloured arrangement, it will make an excellent contribution. It is superb on a pergola or in any position that allows the flowers to be admired from below, and flowers very well in partial shade where its subtle colouring and glistening leaves will be seen at their best.

Rosa 'Claire Jacquier'

Origin: France (Bernaix)
1888
Height: 25ft/7.5m
Z: 5

This Noisette is a bold climber with decorative foliage, marvellous flowers, a good scent and recurrent flowering. It starts to flower in June. Plump creamy yellow buds with pointed sepals open into double apricot-yellow flowers, 3in/8cm across, at first rather cupped, with a lively pattern of packed swirling petals in the middle. As the flowers age they open out fully, becoming paler and showing at the centre a decorative ruff of smaller curved petals framing the stamens. The scent is marvellous – sweet and musky. The flowers are borne in clusters at the tips of long stems, and the foliage is bold and profuse, with attractive bronze new growth and few thorns.

'Claire Jacquier' has many charms. In semi-shade, in a fairly cool position, it will display to best effect its especially beautiful flowers; in a hot sunny site the buds open too quickly and the colour becomes bleached. It is a rose quite sufficiently decorative in itself to require no associated planting, but it looks good with the languid green and white flowers of the summer-flowering *Clematis* 'Alba Luxurians'. In a very large border backed by a wall it would form a superb backdrop to a scheme of yellows, cream and orange.

Rosa 'Constance Spry'

Origin: Britain (Austin) 1961
Height: 7ft/2m
Z: 5

Although a bush, 'Constance Spry' needs much support and is far better grown as a climber. Plump buds fatten up in May, rosy red with ornate sepals, and the flowers open the following month, double, 4 1/2in/11cm across, a rich pink but edged in pale silver-pink. The flowers are beautifully formed, with the outer petals curling backwards and those at the middle swirling about a well-defined centre. They are well scented with a warm spicy perfume. The leaves are very bold, rounded, toothed, with pointed tips.

This is one of the most strikingly handsome of modern roses. With its very large flowers, produced in abundance, and its big, shapely leaves, it is a rose for the bold effect. Because it flowers only once it is probably best in the larger garden where a single wall or fence may be devoted to it. It will flower well in a partly shaded site. Trained sideways it will cover a span of at least 20ft/6m, and in full flower, perhaps forming the dramatic backdrop to a sitting place, it is a marvellous sight. After it has flowered it may be enlivened by training one or two of the later-flowering clematis through its handsome foliage: the August-flowering *Clematis texensis* 'Gravetye Beauty' would be magnificent.

Rosa 'Easlea's Golden Rambler'

Origin: Britain (Easlea)
1932
Height: 15ft/4.5m
Z: 5

This great yellow-flowered Rambler has a splendid fortissimo character. Its buds show red and yellow at first when the sepals begin to part, but the half-open bud – a beautifully scrolled shape – is a warm apricot. The fully open flowers in June are loosely double, 4in/10cm across, creamy yellow. The petals are pleated and rumpled, and as the flowers age they become lavishly blowsy. They have an excellent warm sweet scent, like ripe fruit. The flowers are carried in bold clusters at the tips of long stems, standing well out from the foliage – which is outstanding: dark glossy leaves, rounded and pointed, with strongly marked veins. It is a very healthy and vigorous rose.

'Easlea's Golden Rambler' is bold and brassy but never coarse. Although it flowers only once, its shining foliage will continue to give pleasure. It is superlative on a pergola so that one may look up at its heavy flowers and savour their exceptional perfume to the full. Trained on a wall or trellis its colour would make a marvellous contribution to a border of yellows and creams spread out below it. Because of the large size and forthright colour of its flowers, which would swamp more timid plants, I do not think it is a good idea to mix it with other climbing plants that flower at the same time. But later in the season, some late-summer flowering clematis, such as the mauve 'Little Nell', would look marvellous with it.

Rosa 'Emily Gray'

Origin: Britain (Williams) 1918
Height: 15ft/4.5m
Z: 5

Yellow can be a difficult colour in roses; all too easily, especially in modern varieties, it becomes shrill and overpowering. However, the flowers of the Rambler 'Emily Gray' are an excellent clear lemon-yellow. They open in June from pointed buds gathered in profuse clusters at the tips of stems, semi-double, 3in/8cm across, loosely formed and, with backward-curving petals, becoming splendidly blowsy as they get older. They are very well scented and have prominent stamens. The new growth is a rich red-brown and the holly-like leaves are exceptionally attractive: healthy, glistening like varnish and with strikingly toothed edges.

Although flowering only once – but what a flowering! – 'Emily Gray' earns a prominent place in the garden by virtue of the combination of beautiful flowers and exceptionally decorative foliage. It is an excellent rose for an arbour or for a pergola, especially intermingled with later-flowering climbers such as clematis, which look wonderful against its polished leaves and red stems. The very deeply coloured purple *C.* 'Royal Velours' looks marvellous with it. I have also seen it looking magnificent trained up a large tripod in the centre of a grand border and surrounded by the pale violet spires of *Veronicastrum virginicum*.

Rosa 'Etoile de Hollande, Climbing'

Origin: Netherlands (Verschuren) 1919; climbing form 1931
Height: 18ft/5.5m
Z: 5

Although there are many red roses, few are really good. 'Etoile de Hollande' is an old Hybrid Tea with many outstanding qualities to recommend it. As a bush it has its merits but as a climber it is superlative. Shapely red buds, so dark as to be almost black, open in June into magnificent loosely double red flowers. At first they are deep crimson but as they age they take on a scarlet hue. The flowers remain slightly cupped, 3 1/2in/9cm across, with the outer petals curving back slightly; the texture of the overlapping petals is like that of very fine velvet. Just before collapsing, the flowers become wonderfully voluptuous. Their scent is one of the very best – deep, sweet and vibrant, and after the first show of flowers there will be repeated flowerings throughout the season. The foliage is of the characteristic Hybrid Tea type with bold toothed leaves, but these hang and flutter slightly.

Trained on a wall or trellis at the back of a deep border, 'Etoile de Hollande' would provide a marvellous backdrop to an arrangement of red and purple. But it is a very vigorous grower and among other plants crowded together it may prove difficult to look after. I have grown it on the back wall of a house where it shot up to the upper storeys, giving the lovely experience of beautiful, deliciously scented flowers nodding at one's bedroom window. In all but the coldest gardens it will flower very well on a north wall where its deep colours last much longer.

Rosa 'Félicité Perpétue'

Origin: France (Jacques) 1827
Height: 15ft/4.5m
Z: 5

This splendidly named Rambler celebrates two Carthaginian martyrs, St Felicitas and St Perpetua. Very small red-pink buds open in June to double pompoms of flowers, 2in/5cm across, creamy white but with, here and there, a flush of pink. At first very neatly formed, with regular concentric circles of overlapping petals, they become discreetly blowsy with age and are carried in immense tumbling clusters which give off a light fragrance. The foliage is evergreen, mid green and very healthy, with glistening, elegantly shaped leaflets. It starts to flower late in June and will flower over a very long period. It is a very healthy rose, able to withstand cold weather, and will flower excellently in the shade.

Although vigorous, even boisterous, there is something distinctly feminine about 'Félicité Perpétue'. Its flowers are small and it is important that they should not be too far away – on a wall or fence at the back of a large border they will lose their character and

dissolve in a vague blur of white. The best place to plant it is where its abundant flowers are displayed to best effect and where its charming detail can be properly seen – tumbling over a substantial arbour or framing a doorway in a high wall.

Rosa filipes 'Kiftsgate'

Origin: Britain (Bunyard) 1938
Height: 40ft/11m
Z: 5

This is not a rose for the timid, nor for those short of space. *R. filipes* comes from China and was introduced to western Europe in 1908. The form 'Kiftsgate' was bought from the nurseryman E.A. Bunyard by Miss Heather Muir of Kiftsgate Court in Gloucestershire. It turned out to be superior to the type and is the cultivar universally seen in gardens today. It flowers rather later than most roses, the little globular buds opening in late June. They are borne in immense hanging trusses, often 18in/45cm across and carrying over a hundred flowers, each of which is 1in/2.5cm across, creamy white, with a pronounced tuft of golden stamens. The flowers are slightly cupped and very graceful, perfumed with an intense sweet scent which, when magnified by the profusion of blossom on a mature plant, is one of the most extraordinary scents of any garden plant. The foliage is very striking, pale green with long pointed glistening leaflets. New growth is tinged with bronze. *R. filipes* 'Kiftsgate' flowers only once, though this flowering may continue into August, but its display is by no means finished with the flowers. These are followed by huge quantities of red hips, and in the autumn the leaves turn a marvellous tawny brown.

In the garden of Kiftsgate Court the 'Kiftsgate' rose originally planted by Heather Muir over fifty years ago climbs spectacularly through a copper beech, *Fagus sylvatica* 'Purpurea'. It clearly needs something very big through which to climb, and a large tree is the obvious candidate; it is far too big and wild to be restrained in some neat formal arrangement. It will flower well in partial shade but will take some time to become established under a tree and and will need careful watering when young. However, it is well worth the wait, for it provides, when mature, one of the most marvellous spectacles given by any flowering plant.

Rosa 'Fräulein Octavia Hesse'

Origin: Germany 1909
Height: 12ft/3.6m
Z: 5

This Rambler has something of the character of 'Albéric Barbier' but also has its own distinctive and desirable attributes. Pale lemon-yellow buds open in June to double white flowers, 3 1/2in/9cm across, lavishly informal pompoms, some of which are freckled with pink and suffused with creamy yellow at the centre. When they open fully the flowers resemble handfuls of crumpled satin. They have a delicious sweet and intense scent. The leaves are a gleaming mid green, shapely and finely toothed.

There is a splendidly romantic Belle Epoque flavour to 'Fräulein Octavia Hesse'. The flower colour is attractively muted, not that offensive dead white that can be so oppressive in a garden. The irregular shape of the flowers, with petals crimped and folded, is very ornamental. It is beautiful trained on a fence or wall at the back of a border, with the occasional flowering frond trailing through other plants. It is not too vigorous to be trained up a tripod in the centre of a mixed border. It flowers only once but it makes a good support for other later wall plants. *Eccremocarpus scaber*, with orange flowers and grey-green foliage, is wonderful scrambling through its glistening leaves.

Rosa 'Gloire de Dijon

Origin: France 1853
Height: 12ft/3.6m
Z: 5

'Gloire de Dijon', a climbing Tea, is one of the very finest of the old climbing roses. The shapely buds are tinged with red and, in favoured gardens, will open as early as the beginning of May. The flowers have immense character and charm. They are quartered, double and fully 3in/8cm across, very pale creamy buff, retaining at the tips of the petals some of the red colouring of the buds. The scent is one of the very best, a delicate and lovely Tea rose perfume. After the first early summer flowering it will produce flowers throughout the season. Like many of the best things in life it is not entirely without defects: the foliage is susceptible to black spot, and in humid weather the buds may fail to open. But in full flower it is irresistibly beautiful.

'Gloire de Dijon' in my garden is grown on an old stone wall where it intermingles with the grey foliage of *Buddleja crispa* and with the lilac flowers of the clematis 'Countess of Lovelace'. At the back of a border of creams and yellows it will contribute a warm note. It is especially good trained on a pergola or arch under which one may walk enveloped in its exceptional scent. Also, since the large and weighty flowers have a tendency to hang downwards, they are best displayed where they may be seen from below.

Rosa 'Goldfinch'

Origin: Britain (Paul) 1907
Height: 8ft/2.5m
Z: 5

This small Rambler is the ideal rose for owners of smaller gardens who want the full Rambler experience. Its shapely buds, borne in very profuse clusters at the tips of stems, show a beautiful apricot-yellow as the calyx parts. The flowers, starting in June, are semi-double, a beautiful primrose-yellow at first but

fading to white with a creamy yellow centre,
2 1/2in/6cm across. Petals overlap slightly and the tips
of some are elegantly curled, giving the flower a
particularly attractive shape. A prominent bush of
golden-yellow stamens in the newly opened flowers
turns black as the flower ages. The lavish trusses of
flowers are carried on reddish-brown new growth
bristling with very fine thorns. They give off a light but
very sweet scent, not unlike that of primroses. The
fresh light green foliage has pointed leaflets.

The colour, fragrance, foliage and habit of this
Rambler make it especially valuable for gardens with
restricted space. It flowers only once but it has a long
season. In slight shade its pale colouring will be seen at
its best, but it is excellent on trellis or on a pergola –
where the flowers seen with light shining through them
are especially lovely.

Rosa 'Guinée'

Origin: France (Mallerin)
1938
Height: 15ft/4.5m
Z: 5

This climbing Hybrid Tea produces exquisite,
marvellously scented flowers of a rare deep red. The
plump buds are almost black and open in June into
double flowers of the darkest blood-red, 4in/10cm
across. At first they are slightly cupped, with the outer
petals curving backwards and the inner ones curving
inwards. The texture of the petals is very smooth,
giving them a glistening sheen. As they age the flowers
open out much more loosely but keep their colour

remarkably well. Their perfume is exceptional – rich, sweet and intense. The leaves are boldly shaped and undulating. After its first flowering it will produce scattered flowers throughout the season.

There is no rose, bush or climbing, that can boast of a red to compare with the rich, deep colour of this superlative Hybrid Tea. Its scent, too, is among the very finest. In a former garden I grew it trained on an old pale-grey limestone wall where its colour was superbly displayed. It is best planted alone in a position of prominence so that all attention is focussed on its beauty. Train it, for example, on pale trellis-work to form an arbour surrounding a seat; its scent will be fully appreciated and it will make a breathtaking ornament. It flowers best in a warm sunny position.

Rosa 'Lady Hillingdon, Climbing'

Origin: Britain (Hicks) 1917
Height: 15ft/4.5m
Z: 5

The three outstanding qualities of this climbing Tea rose are its generous bold character, its rare colour and its exquisite scent. Long and pointed buds reveal, when the sepals part, a fresh lemon-yellow, and the partly opened flowers are exquisitely shaped, scrolled, with gracefully unfolding petals. Fully open flowers, in June, are a lovely warm clear apricot-yellow, double in form and 3in/8cm across. They are slightly bell-shaped, hang elegantly and exude an exceptional scent – intense, sweet and spicy. The new growth is a handsome plum colour and the foliage is a fresh glistening green.

'Lady Hillingdon' should be high on the list of

really desirable climbing roses for all those gardeners who can give it the conditions it needs. To perform at its best it demands a warm site, south- or west-facing, and should have the protection of a wall – the perfect wall will have some yellow in its brick or stone. It is marvellous on a pergola, but in all but the warmest gardens may suffer from the windy exposure of such a position. Once you have found the ideal site, any associated planting is superfluous. It will produce flowers intermittently throughout the season and is a rose of such powerful character that it makes a wonderful ornament all on its own.

Rosa 'Lady Waterlow'

Origin: France
(Narbonnand) 1903
Height: 12ft/3.6m
Z: 5

Many of the best climbing Hybrid Tea roses were bred at a time when full-blown romantic character was especially appreciated. 'Lady Waterlow' has all the charm of the turn of the century. Its buds are very beautiful – shapely, pointed and, as the sepals part, revealing a deep blood-red. The flowers in June are semi-double, at first prettily cupped but in time opening out into a flamboyant loose bundle of twisting and overlapping petals. At their largest they are 4 1/2in/11cm across, and their colouring is attractively mixed – a rosy pink at the centre but silver-pink towards the edges, particularly on the backward-curving petals on the outside. Their scent is sweet but faint and there is often a second flowering later in the summer. The foliage is especially striking: lime-green when young, with boldly rounded, toothed and pointed leaflets.

'Lady Waterlow' is healthy and vigorous but not overwhelmingly boisterous. In smaller gardens, trained on a wall or trellis, it its easy to keep within bounds. On the whole I think it is best used by itself for some strikingly decorative purpose; its effusive charms have a tendency to swamp more reticent plants. The sheer glamour of its flowers and the ornamental value of its foliage make it excellent for a bower, giving scented shade to a sitting place.

Rosa laevigata 'Cooperi'

Origin: South east Asia
Height: 20ft/6m
Z: 7

In the right setting this great aristocratic rose is one of the most spectacular of garden plants. It is very vigorous indeed, throwing out strikingly ornamental fleshy new shoots of 7–8ft/2–2.5m in a season – red with bold backward-facing thorns. The single white flowers open from long shapely buds in June. They are 4in/10cm across, with rounded petals and egg-yolk-yellow stamens which become almost black with age. Some of the flowers become speckled with pink as they age. They smell sweetly of cedar wood. Hips form early, pear-shaped and elegant, and in late summer turn orange-yellow. They retain their long, star-shaped sepals and bristle with hairs. The shining healthy leaves are finely edged in red. It may be propagated easily from cuttings. It is a more beautiful rose than the type whose new growth is a more prosaic green.

R. l. 'Cooperi' needs a warm garden, but in conditions that suit it is one of the healthiest of roses. It flowers only once but has a very long season. Its great

vigour and wild character makes this is a rose for the
more informal parts of the garden. I have grown it
successfully scaling an old apple tree under whose
branches it flowered well in dappled shade. It will
scramble through a field hedge from whose top its long
branches will hang festooning it with lavish garlands of
flowers.

Rosa 'Léontine Gervais'

Origin: France (Barbier)
1904
Height: 12ft/3.6m
Z: 5

This vigorous Rambler, of *R. wichuraiana* origins, has
splendidly sumptuous flowers. Its buds are very
ornamental, showing pink and apricot as the sepals
part. The flowers, which open in June, are semi-double,
3in/8cm across, pink with yellow undertones, fading to
creamy white in the sun. The petals are rounded at the
tips and slightly notched, giving a decorative character
to the flower shape. They have an excellent sweet scent.
Flowers are carried in lavish clusters at the tips of long
stems. New shoots are a striking plum colour and the

Illustration opposite:
'Madame Alfred Carrière'

foliage is very distinguished, with shapely little toothed leaflets that have a lively shining surface. In smaller gardens, to keep it within bounds, it may be pruned hard immediately after flowering.

This is not a rose for timid effects – its blowsy abundance should be flaunted. It is admirable trained round an arch or gate, or over a pergola where it will make a scented tunnel and where the flowers are seen to particularly good effect with the sun shining through them. It can, with care, be planted with other roses of very pale pink, such as 'New Dawn', or white with cream undertones, such as 'Madame Alfred Carrière'.

Rosa 'Madame Alfred Carrière'

Origin: France (Schwartz)
1879
Height: 15ft/4.5m
Z: 5

The pink buds of this climbing Noisette open in June into generous double white flowers, 3 1/2in/9cm across, always retaining a hint of creamy pink at the centre. As they become older the flowers become loose and rather dishevelled, taking on the appearance of crushed material. They give off a marvellous deep sweet scent. The foliage has character; it is a fine grey-green with well-shaped rounded and toothed, deeply veined leaves.

The lovely creamy white flowers of 'Madame Alfred Carrière', its generous floriferousness and the exceptional scent make this one of the best climbing roses. After the first flowering it will produce flowers

constantly throughout the season. Although vigorous, it may be pruned as hard as is needed; it flowers on the current year's growth so a spring pruning, quite severe if necessary, is possible. It will be quite happy in semi-shade – I have grown it well on an east-facing wall. Trained round a window, its delicious scent will waft into your room throughout the summer. It will associate very easily with many different plants; I have seen it looking beautiful with the pale lilac-pink late-flowering clematis 'Madame Baron Veillard'. It is very beautiful intermingled with the tender *Buddleja crispa* which has almost white grey felty foliage and racemes of the palest violet flowers.

Rosa 'Madame Caroline Testout, Climbing'

Origin: France
(Pernet-Ducher) 1890
Height: 15ft/4,5m
Z: 5

This sumptuous climbing Hybrid Tea of showy character is among the oldest surviving HT cultivars. Plump buds, the colour of raspberries crushed in cream, open in June into sumptuous, very double heavy flowers, 4in/10cm across, of pale pink with the tips of petals turning even paler. The petals are ruffled, giving lively variations of colour, and the flowers, globe-shaped at first, never open fully. The scent is light but sweet and the leaves are pale green and boldly rounded. It will flower recurrently throughout the season. The growth is rather strong and stiff, and new growth is best curved and trained while it is still pliable.

'Madame Caroline Testout' is vigorous and floriferous. It is a bold, flaunting rose for use where something more timid would not do. Its role in life is to command attention and it should be planted in a prominent position. It is at its best trained high up a wall on its own, fringing upstairs windows. It will do well in part shade; I grew it successfully on a shady west wall where its glowing pink was seen to full effect.

Rosa 'Madame de Sancy de Parabère'

Origin: France (Bonnet)
before 1845
Height: 15ft/4.5m
Z: 5

This Boursault is a substantial climber with large but delicately formed flowers of a marvellous gentle pink. The deep red buds open in May or early June to very big double flowers, 5in/13cm across, an excellent clear pink, with a sweet musky scent. The outer petals are larger than the inner ones, which gives the flower a distinctive shape. The form of the flowers is quite loose, with petals turning hither and thither, giving a sumptuous appearance. They are carried in splendid profusion on entirely thornless wood. The vigorous foliage is very handsome: generous toothed leaves with a leathery surface.

Although flowering only once, 'Madame de Sancy de Parabère' is a marvellous climber. Both its generous flowers which hang heavily down and its floppy leaves, fluttering easily in a slight breeze on the long, whippy new growth, have the same langorous air. It is a magnificent rose for a pergola or arbour in a position where its flowers, swaying on long shoots, may be admired from below. It is in no need of any associated planting; grow it with plants that flower and provide interest in other seasons – clematis, vines or the beautiful golden hop, *Humulus lupulus* 'Aureus'.

Rosa 'Madame Grégoire Staechelin'

Origin: Spain (Dot) 1927
Height: 15ft/4.5m
Z: 5

This Hybrid Tea is one of the most glamorous and superbly scented of all climbing roses. Pale green plump buds open in early June into loosely double flowers 4in/10cm across. They are pale pink with a deeper colour on the backs of the petals, strikingly shown in the newly opened flowers which are slightly cupped. They have a marvellous scent, vibrantly rich and sweet. When the flowers are fully open they assume a voluptuous, languid shape, hanging heavily from their stems. The leaves are mid green and shapely, and new growth is almost thornless. 'Madame Grégoire Staechelin' also produces striking orange hips.

This is a wonderful, glamorous rose. Although I once grew it very successfully in an orchard, scrambling through an apple tree, its sophisticated character makes it better suited to a more formal setting. It is superlative trained on a pergola where its hanging flowers will be well displayed and its scent will be appreciated to the full. Here it may be grown with plants that flower in other seasons, such as wisteria for the spring, late summer-flowering clematis, and vines with lovely autumn colouring such as *Vitis coignetiae*.

Rosa 'Maigold'

Origin: Germany (Kordes)
1953
Height: 12ft/3.6m
Z: 5

'Maigold' is either a shrub with climbing ambitions, or a climber masquerading as a shrub. I include it here because in most gardens its leggy, vigorous growth makes it more suitable as a climber. Long buds with pointed sepals show at first a pink-apricot colour which is carried through into the flowers. These, as the name suggests, open in May. They are huge, over 5in/13cm across, among the largest in span of any rose. But they are very delicately formed and have none of that overstuffed coarseness found in many large-flowered modern roses. They are semi-double, suffused with apricot at first but settling down to a lovely warm butter colour. As the flowers age the petals twist and curl in an exotic way. They have very pronounced golden stamens and a vibrant sweet scent. Their first flowering will last for weeks and there will be subsequent scatterings of flowers throughout the season. The foliage is magnificent, a rich deep green with shining toothed leaves. New growth forms vigorous arching stems bristling with red-brown thorns.

This is a very healthy rose producing large and beautiful well-scented flowers very early in the season. It will flower well in partial shade but would be excellent trained on a tripod or trellis-work tower as the centrepiece for a border with an appropriate colour scheme of buff, cream and yellow. Smaller honeysuckles, such as *Lonicera tragophylla*, also a warm almost orange-yellow, would look magnificent intermingled with the gleaming foliage.

Rosa 'Mermaid'

Origin: Britain (Paul) 1918
Height: 30ft/9m
Z: 5

This is a hybrid between the great Chinese rose, *R. bracteata* and some unknown Tea rose. This parentage has produced a climbing rose that combines wildness and vigour with something more delicate. Striking lemon-yellow buds open in June to stately single pale lemon-yellow flowers, 4in/10cm across with a very prominent tuft of stamens. After the first flowering it will continue to produce flowers intermittently throughout the season, flowering on the current year's growth. The petals overlap slightly and some curl at the edges, giving a lovely graceful appearance, and the flowers have a delicious sweet scent. In all but the warmest gardens it must have a protected position although it will flower in the shade; but in full sun it will flower much more generously. The foliage – evergreen in mild climates – is very handsome, with slender fluttering leaflets. New growth is strikingly flushed with bronze and carries large backward-pointing thorns. It is a very vigorous and healthy rose.

In very warm gardens it is possible to grow 'Mermaid' as a free-standing shrub; it will form a giant mound of thorny stems throwing out quanties of flowers. In most gardens, however, it needs the protection of a wall and a sunny position. It is such an aristocrat, and it produces flowers over such a long season, that it is probably best planted by itself.

Rosa 'Mountain Snow'

Origin: Britain (Austin) 1985
Height: 15ft/4.5m
Z: 5

This new Rambler, bred by David Austin, is one of the very best of the new varieties. It has striking buds frilled with intricate sepals which, as they part, reveal a mixture of pink and cream. The flowers when they open in June are 4in/10cm across, semi-double, ivory-white with hints of cream, with a light sweet scent. The petals have crimped edges and twist gracefully; those at the centre are much smaller and curl over to form a ruff about the golden-yellow stamens. The leaves are a healthy-looking dark green, rounded, slightly toothed and pointed. The new growth is a striking pale green.

'Mountain Snow' is a vigorous rose and its flowers are carried in generous clusters, forming an avalanche of unusually graceful blossom. It is excellent on a pergola where it will be dramatically ornamental in flower, while its handsome foliage will form an

excellent background to plants that flower in other seasons. It would be superb trained on a substantial tripod or trellis obelisk in a large border. It will flower well in partial shade, where its flowers will be seen at their most beautiful, glowing in light shadow.

Rosa 'Mrs Herbert Stevens, Climbing'

Origin: France
(Pernet-Ducher) 1922
Height: 15ft/4.5m
Z: 5

This climbing Hybrid Tea has a marvellous languid character. The fat buds are speckled with pink and the partly open flower in early June is a beautifully formed, scrolled shape, of lovely creamy yellow. The flowers when fully open are cupped but loosely formed, eventually quite blowsy; they are white, semi-double, unusually large, 4 1/2in/11cm across, with a warm cream centre. The outer petals curve backwards sharply but the centres remain neat and scrolled for some time. The heavy flowers, drooping elegantly, hang on their slender stems, and have a delicious sweet scent, smelling slightly of apples. The rather sparse leaves are big, rounded and up to 4in/10cm long. New growth is very vigorous, with thorny wood and leaves strikingly

flushed with bronze-red. After the first summer flowering it will produce scatterings of further flowers throughout the season.

The translucent airy lightness of the petals of the huge flowers of 'Mrs Herbert Stevens' make it one of the most graceful and elegant of climbing roses. It will consort happily with many other climbing plants; I have seen it looking beautiful with the yellow-flowered *Clematis orientalis*, and intermingling with a wall-trained *Ceanothus* 'Gloire de Versailles'. On a pergola its flowers are displayed to special advantage, allowing the light to shine through the petals.

Rosa 'New Dawn'

Origin: USA (Somerset Rose Company) 1930
Height: 10ft/3m
Z: 5

For very good reasons, this Climbing Rose is one of the most popular of 20th-century roses. It appeared as a sport of 'Dr Van Fleet' to which it is identical in all respects except that it is repeat-flowering. Its buds, carried on bronze new growth, have whiskery sepals which separate to show a creamy red. Semi-double

Illustration opposite:
Rosa 'Parkdirektor
Riggers'

flowers open in June and are at first shaped like globes;
the fully open flowers remain still slightly cupped,
3 1/2in/9cm across, very pale, pure pink. They are
carried in generous clusters at the tip of new growth
and have a lovely clear sweet scent. The foliage is an
attractive, shining dark green with very rounded
leaflets, which make an admirable background to the
pink of the flowers. Perpetual flowering, and
performing well in half shade, this climbing rose has
many virtues and no flaws. There is also a good white
form, 'New Dawn, White'.

For the smaller garden 'New Dawn' is an ideal rose.
It is wonderful trained on an arbour over a bench, and
its soft pink will intermingle harmoniously with other
colours: for example with the rich red of *Clematis*
'Gravetye Beauty' or the mauve of *C.* 'Perle d'Azur'.
In a big mixed border, train it on a tall tripod to make a
superb long-flowering ornamental feature. It is also
available trained as a standard.

Rosa 'Parkdirektor Riggers'

Origin: Germany (Kordes)
1957
Height: 12ft/3.6m
Z: 5

A really good clear red is surprisingly rare among
roses. This modern climbing rose is one of the very best
and makes an immensely valuable component of red or
purple planting schemes. The buds are elegantly shaped
and rather pointed, opening in early June into flat,
semi-double flowers, 3in/8cm across, at first deep red
but becoming crimson, with a paler eye and bold

stamens. They are borne more or less continuously throughout the season in clusters at the tips of stems, and the overlapping undulating petals are especially attractive. Later flowers, on current year's growth, are smaller and flatter. It is only very slightly scented. The leaves are handsome: glistening, healthy, rounded and unusually large, up to 3in/8cm long.

The rich red flowers against the dark green foliage of 'Parkdirektor Riggers' are a magnificent sight. Although vigorous it is by no means uncontrollable and may be pruned as severely as needed. Its stiff growth makes it difficult to use on pergolas or arbours and it is at its best trained against a wall. Strong new shoots are easily formed but they tend to stand stiffly out from the wall and should be trained and tied in as soon as they are formed. It will tolerate semi-shade where the flower colour will remain a lovely deep red. With summer-flowering clematis such as the very deep purple 'Royal Velours' growing through it, it makes a sumptuous ornament.

Rosa 'Paul's Himalayan Musk'

Origin: Britain (Paul) 19th century
Height: 30ft/9m
Z: 5

The giant Ramblers, very often with Himalayan blood in them, offer a special kind of pleasure. Their exuberance, scent – magnified by thousands of blossoms – and often beautiful foliage on a grand scale, provide an exhilarating experience. 'Paul's Himalayan Musk', which arose as a seedling of *R. brunonii*, has all these qualities and, in addition, wonderfully decorative delicate flowers. The buds are shapely, with pointed sepals showing pale pink as they open, and are carried at the tips of thin stems in huge clusters. The flowers, which open in June, are pale pink at first, ageing to white touched with pink, loosely double, 1 1/2in/4cm across, and have a sweet piercing scent. The foliage, a glistening grey-green, with leathery toothed leaflets, is very decorative.

This is one of the most beautiful of all the Ramblers but it is not remotely a rose for small gardens or niggling effects. To curb its exuberance would destroy its essence. It will scale a substantial tree, grappling with its boldly pointed thorns and engulfing it in swathes of flowers. If you are lucky enough to have a substantial field hedge it will look very much at home twining through old hawthorn, holly or elder.

Rosa 'Phyllis Bide'

Origin: Britain (Bide)
1923
Height: 12ft/3.6m
Z: 5

This relatively small Rambler of unknown parentage has flowers that cannot be mistaken for those of any other rose. Beautiful creamy pink buds open in June into little cupped flowers of ivory and clear pink. The petals curl back and are scrolled round the centre. They then open fully into double flowers, 3in/8cm across, of potentially disastrous colouring: yellow at the centre becoming pink at the tips. But this unique cocktail of colours produces in fact a charming effect, merging at a distance ino a warm rose-cream. The flowers are produced in prodigal abundance, their petals intricately curled and crimped in a very decorative way, and have a faint sweet scent. The foliage is elegant with very attractive dark green leaves with a shining, leathery surface.

The unusual colour of 'Phyllis Bide' does not associate easily and I would hesitate to mix it with other plants. Among the Ramblers it is relatively small and easy to keep in control, making it especially valuable for smaller gardens. It will flower repeatedly throughout the season, deep into the autumn, and is the ideal rose to train on a wall or fence in some position where a perpetual summer ornament would be particularly appreciated: opposite a kitchen window, for example. It will flower well in the semi-shade.

Rosa 'Pompon de Paris, Climbing'

Origin: bush form, 1839
Height: 10ft/3m
Z: 5

This is a climbing form of a miniature China rose of the type which was widely used in the 19th century for growing in pots. Its buds are borne in clusters which open in June into rosettes, 1 1/2in/4cm across, of a striking lilac-pink. As the flowers age they become more loosely double and change colour to a rosy pink. The undulating petals are slightly frilly and towards the centre of the flower they are smaller and curve attractively inwards. The foliage is delicate and fern-like, with little finely toothed leaves of a decorative grey-green. New growth is made on quite short, practically thornless stems. Older plants become rather twiggy and dense, giving them great character.

This very decorative climber must have a protected, sunny position to give of its best. It flowers only once (unlike the original bush form which is perpetual-flowering) but produces its flowers in wonderful abundance. In full flower it is a splendid sight, its great charm lying in the combination of miniature flowers and lavish profusion. Its decorative foliage makes an excellent support for summer-flowering clematis later in the season. The twiggy growth is best pruned over in the early spring, which will both tidy it up and encourage new flowering growth later in the year.

Rosa 'Rambling Rector'

Origin: Britain before 1912
Height: 20ft/6m
Z: 5

This giant Rambler of mysterious origins is often rather cavalierly dismissed as being useful only to conceal unsightly buildings. In fact it has many other virtues. It is immensely floriferous, its lavish clusters of frilly little buds bursting into flower in June and filling the air with an intoxicating fragrance. The flowers are semi-double, 1 1/2in/4cm creamy white at first, and increasingly yellow towards the centre where the prominent stamens are egg-yolk-yellow. As the flowers age they become almost pure white and the stamens much darker, making a circle of black spots in the centre. The petals are loosely heart-shaped and some have frilly edges. One of the charms of 'Rambling Rector' is that buds and flowers at various stages of evolution are simultaneously displayed. The foliage is grey-green with neat pointed and finely toothed leaflets. It has a fine display of hips in the autumn, gleaming little spheres of orange-yellow, which look beautiful among the yellowing autumn foliage.

'Rambling Rector' will ramble freely over walls, buildings and other large plants where it will display the wilder side of its nature. Space permitting, it may also be grown as a free-standing shrub to form an immense mound which would make a magnificent feature in the wild garden. But I have also seen it beautifully trained along a long 7ft/2m high wall in a formal garden, where summer-flowering clematis added their flowers later in the season.

Rosa 'Russelliana'

Origin: Spain (?) 1840
Height: 15ft/4.5m
Z: 5

Some gardeners find this Rambler rather coarse; I find it cheerful and decorative. Its buds are ornamental, fat little globes frilled with ornate sepals and showing rich deep red as they start to open. The flowers in June, borne in generous clusters at the tips of stems, are double, lilac-crimson fading to rosy purple with hints of magenta, 2in/5cm across. They have a musky scent. The petals are folded and overlapping, giving the flowers an air of animation. The leaves are rounded and toothed, and pale green new growth has fine red thorns.

Good taste in gardening is too often associated with subdued colours and dull effects. 'Russelliana' at the height of its flowering, with buds and flowers in different shades of red and purple according to their evolution, presents an invigorating sight – like an appetising dessert make from crushed berries. It is a tough vigorous rose which will make a decorative contribution in an awkward spot. It will do well in the shade and is very resistant to disease. Bolder gardeners will mix it with a summer-flowering clematis – one of the dark purple cultivars of *C. viticella*, for example – to make a heady mixture of red and purple.

Rosa 'Sanders' White Rambler'

Origin: Britain (Sanders)
1912
Height: 15ft/4.5m
Z: 5

In every way this is one of the best of the Ramblers, flowering rather late in the season, at the end of June and into July. The flowers are carried in wonderful profusion; clusters of shapely pale yellow pointed buds open into double white rosettes with a pale creamy yellow centre, 2 1/2in/6cm across. The petals are quite loosely held, have scalloped tips and overlap; at the centre of the flowers the petals are quite small and curl round to frame the very striking golden-yellow stamens. The flowers have a marvellous clear sweet scent which becomes fortissimo when the rose is fully in flower. The foliage is especially fine, with gleaming fresh green leaflets, elegantly pointed.

This is one of the most beautiful of all decorative climbing plants. It flowers only once but it continues for some weeks, and the harmony of the details – delicate flowers, fine foliage and delicious scent – make it exceptional. Although a substantial plant, it may be kept under control by pruning vigorously after flowering. It is at its best alone, covering a wall or, better still, since it has a tendency to attract mildew, on an arbour. A cool, partly shaded site will suit it well, emphasising the pale flowers and glistening foliage.

Rosa 'Seagull'

Origin: Britain (Pritchard) 1907
Height: 20ft/6m
Z: 5

This large and vigorous Rambler has flowers of lovely delicacy. The buds, carried in lavish clusters, are pale lemon-yellow and cone-shaped, with an elegant little ruff of pointed sepals at the base. The flowers in June are semi-double, white, 1 1/2in/4cm across, with a very large cluster of stamens whose golden colour suffuses the centre of the flowers. As they age the stamens lose their colour and the flowers become completely white. They are sweetly scented, with a hint of cloves. The petals overlap and are informally arranged, giving the flowers, despite their small size, much character. It has beautiful foliage with elegant grey-green pointed leaflets.

At the height of its flowering few Ramblers are more spectacular than 'Seagull'; the abundance of flowers completely obscures the leaves, making an avalanche of white flecked with gold. I have seen it very successfully trained on a pergola, forming lavish garlands between the uprights, with late summer-flowering clematis and the golden-leafed hop,

Humulus lupulus 'Aureus', to provide interest once
'Seagull's' single flowering was over. But it is a versatile
rose and would be equally at home rambling
unconstrained through an old apple tree in the orchard.

Rosa 'Sombreuil, Climbing'

Origin: France (Robert)
1850
Height: 10ft/3m
Z: 5

This old climbing Tea rose produces sumptuous
flowers of an old-fashioned character. They open in
June, very double, 4 1/2in/11cm across, and are white
with a creamy pink centre. The petals are packed into a
loosely quartered pattern but are folded and
undulating, giving the texture of pleated satin. They
have a marvellous rich clean scent. The foliage is bold
and handsome, with glistening grey-green slightly
toothed leaves. It is especially hardy for a Tea rose.

This is one of the most dramatically beautiful of all
climbing roses, and few modern roses have such
character. Originally a bush, it is far better as a climber;
the generous repeat-flowering blooms are so heavy that
they are much better displayed above eye level. In
protected gardens it is especially good on a pergola

Illustration opposite:
Rosa 'Souvenir de la
Malmaison, Climbing'

where all its details may be admired from close up. It is
easy to keep under control and in smaller gardens, in
which its repeat-flowering will be particularly valued, is
the perfect rose to train over a terrace or sitting place. It
is on the whole planted by itself; it will overwhelm
more timid plants.

Rosa 'Souvenir de la Malmaison, Climbing'

Origin: Britain (Bennett)
1893
Height: 10ft/3m
Z: 5

This started as a climbing sport of the older 'Souvenir
de la Malmaison', a Bourbon rose raised in France in
1843, but since the big heavy flowers tend to nod
downwards and are therefore best seen from below, the
climbing version is preferable to the bush. From plump
rosy buds – very beautiful when half open – the flowers
emerge in June, 3 1/2in/9cm across, fully double, an
exquisite pale creamy pink, deeper towards the centre,
with packed, fragile petals. It has mid green foliage with
rounded and toothed leaflets. The scent is rather
mysterious, not sweet, and smelling of wine. In full
bloom it is one of the most spectacular roses there is.
It must have a sunny protected position and its great
enemy, as with other Bourbons, is wet weather; the best
examples I have seen are in gardens with low rainfall. It
will usually produce a second flush of flowers in late
summer.

 This is a rose that is best displayed alone or in some
very simple setting. Trained over an arbour, providing a
lovely canopy to a seat, it has breathtaking presence. In
French formal rose gardens it is sometimes seen
beautifully trained on a tall metal frame.

Rosa 'Souvenir du Docteur Jamain'

Origin: France (Lacharme)
1865
Height: 8ft/2.5m
Z: 5

This Hybrid Perpetual is a shrub but it has such a lax
habit, and throws out such long thin shoots, that it is
much better used as a climber. Its buds are produced in
clusters, and when the sepals part they reveal a vivid
deep red. The flowers, opening in June, are double,
3in/8cm across, of a marvellous and exotic colour: very
deep rich maroon with the texture of velvet. Their scent
is among the very best – rich and spicy. The flowers are
loosely cupped and the petals swirl hither and thither.

The foliage is mid green with shapely leaflets, rounded and toothed. Bright sunlight will cause the flowers to discolour, becoming a brown-red, like red wine that is past its prime. To preserve their deep and beautiful colour the plant should be in a shady position, never on a south-facing wall. It will produce a good second show of flowers in the autumn.

The deep purple of the flowers and their fabulous scent are what make 'Souvenir du Docteur Jamain' special. It will probably be easiest to find the shady site that it enjoys on a wall, but I have seen it very successfully trained on a large wooden tripod at the centre of a grand mixed border. Its deep colour will make a dazzling and long-lasting contribution to a scheme of red and purple.

Rosa 'Zéphirine Drouhin'

Origin: France (Bizot)
1868
Height: 10ft/3m
Z: 5

'Zéphirine Drouhin', a climbing Bourbon, is unlike any other rose and, once seen, cannot be forgotten. Bold, plump red buds open in June into sumptuous loosely double flowers, 3 1/2in/9cm across, a sprightly cerise-pink fading to a silver-pink. The petals are slightly frilly at the tip, often curling over to reveal

their paler underside. Although the petals are not very numerous, their twisting shape gives the flowers a generous fullness. They give off a rich deep scent. After the profuse flowering in June, scatterings of flowers are produced more or less continuously throughout the season. The foliage is pale green, bold and shapely. There are no thorns.

It is the whole effect of 'Zéphirine Drouhin' that is most memorable, though the profusion of slightly sharp pink flowers, scattered along the length of long upright thornless shoots, and the perpetual delicious wafts of scent are what stick in the mind. It is quite happy in semi-shade where the liveliness of colour will be better preserved. It may also be grown as a very substantial bush; in this form it will make a spectacular long-term border ornament. A sport of 'Zéphirine Drouhin', 'Kathleen Harrop' (1919) is similar in all respects except that its slightly less double flowers are a shell-pink. It too produces a profusion of flowers from June to the autumn.

Illustration: 'Albéric Barbier'

Roses by Colour

Roses are listed here according to their colour of flowers. They are chosen for their particularly beautiful flowers in each colour, grouped separately for bush roses and climbers.

PINK

Bush Roses
'Abbotswood'
'Ardoisée de Lyon'
'Baronne Prévost'
'Belle Amour'
'Bourbon Queen'
'Celsiana'
'Complicata'
'Comte de Chambord'
'Fantin-Latour'
'Glamis Castle'
'Great Maiden's Blush'
'Ispahan'
R. nutkana 'Plena'
'René d'Anjou'
'Stanwell Perpetual'

Climbers
'Albertine'
'Constance Spry'
'Lady Waterlow'
'Madame Caroline Testout, Climbing'
'Madame Grégoire Staechelin'
'New Dawn'
'Zéphirine Drouhin'

WHITE

Bush Roses
R. × *alba* 'Alba Maxima'
'Blanche Double de Coubert'
'Boule de Neige'
'Frau Karl Druschki'
'Madame Hardy'
'Madame Legras de Saint Germain'
'Nevada'
'Nyveldt's White'
'Paulii'
'Pax'
'Schneezwerg'

Climbers
'Albéric Barbier'
R. banksiae var. *banksiae*
R. bracteata
R. brunonii 'La Mortola'
'City of York'
R. filipes 'Kiftsgate'
R. laevigata 'Cooperi'
'Madame Alfred Carrière'
'Mountain Snow'
'Mrs Herbert Stevens'
'Sanders' White Rambler'
'Seagull'
'Sombreuil, Climbing'

Illustration: 'Goldfinch'

PURPLE/CRIMSON

Bush Roses
'Alain Blanchard'
'Cerise Bouquet'
'Charles de Mills'
'De Rescht'
'Madame Delaroche-Lambert'
'Nuits de Young'
'Prince Charles'
'Roseraie de l'Haÿ'
'Tuscany Superb'
'William Lobb'
'Zigeunerknabe'

Climbers
'Bleu Magenta'
'Blush Noisette'
'Souvenir du Docteur Jamain'

RED

Bush Roses
R. moyesii
'Robert le Diable'
'Scharlachglut'

Climbers
'Etoile de Hollande, Climbing'
'Guinée'
'Parkdirektor Riggers'

YELLOW/APRICOT

Bush Roses
'Buff Beauty'
'Canary Bird'
'Frühlingsgold'
'Golden Wings'
R. × harisonii
R. xanthina hugonis

Climbers
'Alister Stella Gray'
R. banksiae 'Lutea'
'Céline Forestier'
'Claire Jacquier'
'Easlea's Golden Rambler'
'Emily Gray'
'Gloire de Dijon'
'Goldfinch'
'Lady Hillingdon'
'Maigold'
'Mermaid'

ROSES WITH PARTI-COLOURED FLOWERS
'Baron Girod de
  l'Ain' (crimson/white)
'Camaïeux' (pink/purple)
'Commandant de
  Beaurepaire' (pink/purple)
'Ferdinand Pichard'
  (white/crimson)
R. gallica 'Versicolor'
  (pink/crimson)
'Honorine de
  Brabant' (pink/purple)
'Perle des Panachées'
  (white/purple)
'Tricolore de Flandre'
  (pink/purple)
'Variegata di Bologna'
  (pink/crimson)

Roses with Good Foliage

Bush Roses
R. × *alba* 'Alba Maxima'
R. *eglanteria*
R. *fedtschenkoana*
'Fru Dagmar Hastrup'
R. *glauca*
'Great Maiden's Blush'
'Greenmantle'
'Heather Muir'
R. × *jacksonii* 'Max Graf'
R. *nutkana* 'Plena'
'Nyveldt's White'
'Roseraie de l'Haÿ'
'Schneezwerg'
R. *xanthina hugonis*
'Wolley-Dod'

Climbers
'Aimée Vibert'
'Albéric Barbier'
'Bobbie James'
R. *bracteata*
R. *brunonii* 'La Mortola'
'City of York'
'Easlea's Golden Rambler'
'Emily Gray'
R. *filipes* 'Kiftsgate'
R. *laevigata* 'Cooperi'
'Maigold'
'Sanders' White Rambler'

Roses for Small Gardens

For smaller gardens perpetual flowering roses of modest size are especially valuable. These are among the best, grouped as bushes and climbers, with flower colours indicated in each case.

Bush Roses
(up to 5ft/1.5m high)
'Ardoisée de Lyon' (pink)
'Cécile Brünner' (pink)
'Comte de Chambord' (pink)
'De Rescht' (purple)
'Felicia' (pink)
'Gertrude Jekyll' (pink)
'Glamis Castle' (white)
'Gruss an Aachen' (pink)
'Hermosa' (pink)
'Iceberg' (white)
'Kathryn Morley' (pink)
'Le Havre' (pink)
'Marchesa Boccella' (pink)
'Mary Rose' (pink)
'Mevrouw Nathalie
    Nypels' (pink)
'Reine des Violettes' (purple)
'Salet' (pink)
'The Countryman' (pink)
'White Pet' (white)
'Winchester Cathedral' (white)

Climbers
(up to 12ft/3.6m high)
'Blush Noisette' (purple)
'Céline Forestier' (yellow)
'New Dawn' (pink)
'Souvenir du Docteur
    Jamain' (purple)
'Zéphirine Drouhin' (pink)

Illustration: 'Souvenir
de la Malmaison'

Roses with Exceptional Scent

The scent of roses, one of their most valued qualities, is famously difficult to describe. Those listed below are by common consent among the most deliciously perfumed roses. Their scent is often at its best in cool or damp weather.

Bush Roses
'Ardoisée de Lyon'
'Assemblage des Beautés'
'Boule de Neige'
'Buff Beauty'
'Comte de Chambord'
'Conrad Ferdinand Meyer'
'De Rescht'
'Great Maiden's Blush'
'Honorine de Brabant'
'Madame Isaac Pereire'
'Madame Zöetmans'
'Mevrouw Nathalie Nypels'

'Guinée'
'Lady Hillingdon, Climbing'
'Madame Alfred Carrière'
'Madame Caroline Testout'
'Madame Grégoire Staechelin'
'Mrs Herbert Stevens'
'Souvenir de la Malmaison'
'Souvenir du Docteur Jamain'

Climbers
'Albertine'
'Alister Stella Gray'
'*R. banksiae* var. *banksiae*
'Céline Forestier'
'City of York'
'Etoile de Hollande, Climbing'
'Gloire de Dijon'

Roses for Shade

Almost all roses will flower better in full sun than they will in full shade. However, there are many that will flower well in part shade – either the dappled shade of a light canopy or in a position where they will receive sunlight for only part of the day. Some roses, whose flower colour – dark reds or purples, for example – may be harmed by full sunshine, will be much more beautiful in such a position. All the following will do well in part shade.

Bush Roses
'Abbotswood'
'Alain Blanchard'
'Amy Robsart'
'Assemblage des Beautés'
'Blanche Double de Coubert'
'Bourbon Queen'
'Buff Beauty'
'Canary Bird'
'Cerise Bouquet'
'Complicata'
'Conrad Ferdinand Meyer'
'Cornelia'

'De Rescht'
'Duchesse de Montebello'
R. eglanteria
'Fimbriata'
'Fru Dagmar Hastrup'
R. × francofurtana
'Frühlingsanfang'
'Frühlingsgold'
R. glauca
'Gloire de France'
'Great Maiden's Blush'
'Greenmantle'
'Heather Muir'

'Hebe's Lip'
'Honorine de Brabant'
R. × jacksonii 'Max Graf'
'Madame Hardy'
'Madame Isaac Pereire'
'Madame Legras de Saint
    Germain'
'Madame Plantier'
'Marguerite Hilling'
R. moyesii
R. nutkana 'Plena'
'Nyveldt's White'
'Pax'
'Penelope'
'Petite Lisette'
R. pimpinellifolia
'Pompon Blanc Parfait'
'Prince Charles'
'Raubritter'
'Roseraie de l'Haÿ'
'Scharlachglut'
'Schneezwerg'
'Souvenir de Philémon Cochet'
R. villosa
'Wolley-Dod'
'Zigeunerknabe'

Climbers
'Albéric Barbier'
'Alister Stella Gray'
'Bleu Magenta'
'Blush Noisette'
'Bobbie James'
R. brunonii 'La Mortola'

'City of York'
'Claire Jacquier'
'Easlea's Golden Rambler'
'Etoile de Hollande, Climbing'
R. filipes 'Kiftsgate'
'Goldfinch'
'Léontine Gervais'
'Madame Alfred Carrière'
'Madame de Sancy de
    Parabère'
'Mermaid'
'Parkdirektor Riggers'
'Paul's Himalayan Musk'
'Phyllis Bide'
'Sanders' White Rambler'
'Souvenir du Docteur Jamain'

Illustration: 'Easlea's
Golden Rambler'

Roses for Informal Places

Species roses, and roses of wild character, are sometimes suitable for borders within the garden. But they are often at their best in orchards, woodland and less formal places. The following are roses that are most appropriate for the wilder parts of the garden.

Bush Roses	Climbing Roses
'Abbotswood'	'Bobbie James'
'Cerise Bouquet'	*R. bracteata*
R. eglanteria	*R. brunonii* 'La Mortola'
'Frühlingsanfang'	*R. laevigata* 'Cooperi'
'Frülingsgold'	'Maigold'
R. glauca	'Paul's Himalayan Musk'
'Macrantha'	'Rambling Rector'
'Marguerite Hilling'	'Seagull'
R. moyesii	
'Nevada'	
R. nutkana 'Plena'	
R. pimpinellifolia	
'Scharlachglut'	
R. stella mirifica	
R. xanthina hugonis	

Roses for Structure

Many roses form bushes of striking form which make them valuable structural plants, giving shape to the border or providing an eyecatcher to terminate a vista. Some form stately upright bushes, such as 'Great Maiden's Blush', others handsomely rounded shapes, like *R. × jacksonii* 'Max Graf'.

R. × alba 'Alba Maxima'	'Königin von Dänemark'
'Amy Robsart'	'Madame Hardy'
'Blanche Double de Coubert'	'Madame Legras de Saint
'Céleste'	Germain'
R. fedtschenkoana	'Marguerite Hilling'
'Frühlingsgold'	*R. moyesii*
R. glauca	'Nevada'
'Golden Wings'	*R. nutkana* 'Plena'
'Great Maiden's Blush'	'Nyveldt's White'
'Heather Muir'	*R. × odorata* 'Mutabilis'
'Henry Martin'	'Roseraie de l'Haÿ'
'Honorine de Brabant'	'Scharlachglut'
R. × jacksonii 'Max Graf'	*R. stellata mirifica*

Reading List

General and Historical

John Fisher *The Companion to Roses* (1986)

Michael Gibson *The Rose Gardens of England* (1988)

Gertrude Jekyll and Edward Mawley *Roses for English Gardens* (1902)

Roger Philips and Martyn Rix *Roses* (1988)

Roger Philips and Martyn Rix *The Quest for the Rose* (1993)

Graham Stuart Thomas *The Old Shrub Roses* (1955)

Graham Stuart Thomas *Shrub Roses of Today* (1962)

Graham Stuart Thomas *Climbing Roses Old and New* (1965)

Graham Stuart Thomas *An English Rose Garden* (1991)

Graham Stuart Thomas *The Graham Stuart Thomas Rose Book* (1994)

Reference Books

David Austin *The Heritage of the Rose* (1988)

Peter Beales *Roses* (1992)

W.J. Bean *Trees and Shrubs Hardy in the British Isles* (4 volumes 1970–80; supplement, 1988)

Brent C. Dickerson *The Old Rose Advisor* (1992)

Gerd Krüssmann *Roses* (1982)

Trevor Griffiths *My World of Roses* (1986)

Hardiness Zones

Temperature Ranges		
F	Zone	C
below −50	1	below −45
−50 to −40	2	−45 to −40
−40 to −30	3	−40 to −34
−30 to −20	4	−34 to −29
−20 to −10	5	−29 to −23
−10 to 0	6	−23 to −17
0 to 10	7	−17 to −12
10 to 20	8	−12 to −7
20 to 30	9	−7 to −1
30 to 40	10	−1 to 5

Hardiness zones are based on the average annual minimum temperature in different areas, graded from Zone 1, the coldest, to Zone 10, the warmest; thus, if a plant has the rating Zone 7 it will not dependably survive in a zone of a lower number. But the data are only broadly relevant and are more valid for continental climates than for maritime ones. In Britain and many parts of Europe, for example, local microclimate rather than the hardiness zone band is more likely to determine a plant's hardiness. It should also be said that a plant's chances of survival may be influenced by other things than temperature; drainage, rain, amount of sunshine and protection from winds may make a fundamental difference.

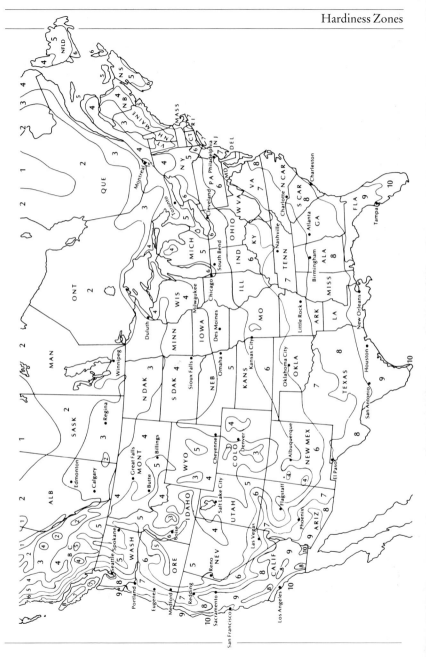

Index

Note: Cultivars are indexed under the cultivar name, e.g. 'Abbotswood'. Species and hybrids are indexed under *Rosa* followed by the specific name.

'Abbotswood' 38–9
'Adélaïde d'Orléans' 186–7
'Aimée Vibert' 187
'Alain Blanchard' 39
Alba roses 12–13
'Albéric Barbier' 187–8
'Albertine' 188–90
'Alister Stella Gray' 190–1
'Amy Robsart' 79
Apothecaries' Rose, The see *R. gallica* var. *officinalis*
'Ardoisée de Lyon' 41
'Assemblage des Beautés' 42
Autumn damask see *R. × damascena semperflorens*

'Baron Girod de l'Ain' 42–4
'Baronne Prévost' 44–5
'Belle Amour' 45–6
'Belle de Crécy' 46–7
'Belle Isis' 47–8
'Bizarre Triomphant' see 'Charles de Mills'
'Blairii Number One' 193–4
'Blairii Number Two' 193–4
'Blanche Double de Coubert' 48–9
'Bleu Magenta' 194–5
'Blush Noisette' 195–6
'Blush Rambler' 196–7
'Bobbie James' 197–8
'Bonica' 49–50
'Boule de Neige' 50
'Bourbon Queen' 51–2
Bourbon roses 13
'Buff Beauty' 52

'Camaïeux' 53
'Canary Bird' 54–5
'Capitaine Basroger' 55–6

'Cécile Brünner' 56–7
'Cécile Brünner, Climbing' 57
'Cécile Brünner, White' 57
'Céleste' 57–8
'Céline Forestier' 200–2
'Celsiana' 58
Centifolia roses 14
'Cerise Bouquet' 60
'Chapeau de Napoléon' see *R. × centifolia* 'Cristata'
'Charles de Mills' 60–2
China roses 14
'City of York' 202–3
'Claire Jacquier' 203–4
Climbing roses 15
'Commandant Beaurepaire' 62–3
'Complicata' 63–4
'Comte de Chambord' 64–6
'Conrad Ferdinand Meyer' 66
'Constance Spry' 204–5
'Cornelia' 66–7
'Coupe d'Hébé' 68–9
'Cuisse de Nymphe' see 'Great Maiden's Blush'

Damask roses 15
'De Meaux' 70–1
'De Meaux, White' 71
'De Rescht' 71
'Dembrowski' 72–3
'Direktor Benschop' see 'City of York'
'Du Maître d'Ecole' 73–4
'Duchess of Portland' see 'Portlandica'
'Duchesse de Buccleugh' 74–5
'Duchesse de Montebello' 76
'Duchesse de Verneuil' 77–8
'Dunwich Rose' 155

'Easlea's Golden Rambler' 205–6
'Emily Gray' 206–7

'Empress Josephine' see *R.* ×
 francofurtana
'Etoile de Hollande,
 Climbing' 207–8

'Fantin-Latour' 79–80
'Fée des Neiges' see 'Iceberg'
'Felicia' 81–2
'Félicité Parmentier' 82–3
'Félicité Perpétue' 208–9
'Ferdinand Pichard' 84
'Fimbriata' 84–6
Floribunda roses 15
'Frau Karl Druschki' 88–9
'Fräulein Octavia Hesse'
 210–11
'Fritz Nobis' 89–90
'Fru Dagmar Hastrup' 90–1
'Frühlingsanfang' 91–2
'Frühlingsgold' 92–3

Gallica roses 15–16
'Gertrude Jekyll' 95–6
'Glamis Castle' 96–7
'Gloire de Dijon' 211–12
'Gloire de France' 98–9
'Golden Wings' 99
'Goldfinch' 212–13
'Great Maiden's Blush'
 100–1
'Greenmantle' 79
'Gros Choux de Hollande'
 101–2
'Gruss an Aachen' 102–3
'Guinée' 213–14
'Gypsy Boy' see
 'Zigeunerknabe'

'Heather Muir' 103–4
'Hebe's Lip' 104–5
'Henri Fouquier' 105–6
'Henri Martin' 106–7
'Hermosa' 107–8
'Honorine de Brabant' 108–9
Hybrid Musk roses 16
Hybrid Perpetual roses 16
Hybrid Tea roses 16–18

'Iceberg' 109–10
'Iceberg, Climbing' 109–10
'Impératrice Joséphine' see
 R. × *francofurtana*
'Ispahan' 110–12

Jacobite rose, see *R.* × *alba*
 'Alba Maxima'
Jacques, Antoine 11
'Jacques Cartier' see
 'Marchesa Boccella'
'James Mitchell' 113–14
'Jeanne de Montfort' 114–15
'Jennie Duval' see 'Président
 de Sèze'
Josephine, Empress 11,15,87

'Kathryn Morley' 115–16
Kiftsgate Court 101, 145–6,
 168
Kiftsgate rose see *R. filipes*
 'Kiftsgate'
'Königin von Dänemark'
 116–17
Kordes Söhne 11–12

'La Belle Distinguée' 117
La Malmaison 11,87
La Mortola 200
'La Noblesse' 118–19
'La Petite Duchesse' see 'La
 Belle Distinguée'
'La Reine Victoria' see
 'Reine Victoria'
'La Ville de Bruxelles'
 119–20
'Lady Hillingdon,
 Climbing' 214–15
'Lady Waterlow' 215–16
'Le Havre' 120–1
'Leda' 121–2
Lee & Kennedy 11
'Léontine Gervais' 217–18
Lindsay, Nancy 45
'Little White Pet' see 'White
 Pet'
'Louise Odier' 122–3

Macartney Rose, The see *R. bracteata*
'Macrantha' 123–4
'Madame Alfred Carrière' 218–20
'Madame Caroline Testout, Climbing' 220–1
'Madame de Sancy de Parabère' 221–2
'Madame Delaroche-Lambert' 124–5
'Madame Grégoire Staechelin' 222–3
'Madame Hardy' 125–6
'Madame Hébert' see 'Président de Sèze'
'Madame Isaac Pereire' 126–7
'Madame Lauriol de Barny' 127–8
'Madame Legras de Saint Germain' 128–9
'Madame Neumann' see 'Hermosa'
'Madame Knorr' see 'Comte de Chambord'
'Madame Pierre Oger' 129–30
'Madame Plantier' 130–1
'Madame Zöetmans' 131–2
'Maigold' 223–4
'Marchesa Boccella' 132–3
'Marguerite Hilling' 133–4
'Mary Rose' 134–6
'Max Graf' see *R. × jacksonii*
'Max Graf'
'Mélanie Lemaire' see 'Hermosa'
'Mermaid' 224–5
'Mevrouw Nathalie Nypels' 134–6
'Monthly Rose' see *R. × odorata* 'Pallida'
Moss roses 18
'Mountain Snow' 225–6
'Mrs Doreen Pike' 138–9
'Mrs Herbert Stevens, Climbing' 226–7
'Mrs John Laing' 139
'Mrs William Paul' 139–40
'Mutabilis' see *R. × odorata* 'Mutabilis'

'Nathalie Nypels' see 'Mevrouw Nathalie Nypels'
'Nevada' 140–2
'New Dawn' 227–8
'Noisette Carnée' see 'Blush Noisette'
Noisette roses 18
'Nuits de Young' 142–3
'Nyveldt's White' 144–5

'Oeillet Flamand' see 'Oeillet Parfait'
'Oeillet Parfait' 146–7
'Old Black' see 'Nuits de Young'
'Old Blush China' see *R. × odorata* 'Pallida'
'Old Velvet' see 'Tuscany Superb'

'Painted Damask' see 'Leda'
'Parkdirektor Riggers' 228–30
'Parson's Pink' see *R. × odorata* 'Pallida'
Paul & Son 11
'Paulii' 147–8
'Paulii Rosea' 148
'Paul's Himalayan Musk' 230–1
'Pax' 149–50
'Penelope' 150
'Perle des Panachées' 150–2
'Petite de Hollande' 152–3
'Petite Lisette' 153–4
'Phyllis Bide' 231–2
Polyantha roses 18
'Pompon Blanc Parfait' 156
'Pompon de Paris, Climbing' 232–3

'Pompon des Dames' see
 'Perle des Panachées'
'Pompon des Princes' see
 'Ispahan'
Portland Rose see
 'Portlandica'
Portland roses 18–19
'Portlandica' 157–8
'Président de Sèze' 158–9
'Prince Charles' 159–60

'Quatre Saisons' see R. ×
 damascena semperflorens
'Queen of Denmark' see
 'Königin von Dänemark'

Rambler roses 19
'Rambling Rector' 233–4
'Raubritter' 160–1
'Red Moss' see 'Henri
 Martin'
'Reine des Violettes' 161–2
'Reine Victoria' 162–3
'René d'Anjou' 163–4
'Robert le Diable' 164–5
Rosa × alba 12
 R. × a. 'Alba Maxima'
  39–40
 R. × a. 'Semiplena' 40
R. banksiae var. banksiae
 191–2
 R. b. 'Lutea' 192–3
R. bracteata 198–9
R. brunonii 199–200
 R. b. 'La Mortola' 199–200
R. californica 'Plena' see R.
 nutkana 'Plena'
R. canina
R. × centifolia 'Cristata'
 59–60
R. × damascena
 semperflorens 69–70
R. eglanteria 78–9
R. fedtschenkoana 80–1
R. filipes 'Kiftsgate' 209–10
R. foetida 'Persiana' 86–7
R. × francofurtana 87

R. gallica 15
 R. g. var. officinalis 11,
  93–4
 R. g. 'Versicolor' 15,94–5
R. glauca 97–8
R. × harisonii 155
R. × jacksonii 'Max Graf'
 112–13
R. laevigata 'Cooperi'
 216–17
R. moyesii 136–7
 R. m. 'Geranium' 137
 R. m. 'Sealing Wax' 137
R. nutkana 'Plena' 143–4
R. × odorata 'Mutabilis'
 145–6
 R. × odorata 'Pallida' 146
R. pimpinellifolia 154–5
 R. p. 'Grandiflora' 155
R. rubiginosa see R.
 eglanteria
R. rubrifolia see R. glauca
R. sericea 103
R. spinosissima see R.
 pimpinellifolia
R. stellata mirifica 171–2
R. turkestanica see R. ×
 odorata 'Mutabilis'
R. villosa 178–9
R. xanthina hugonis 182–3
Rosa Mundi 15,94
'Rose de Meaux' see 'De
 Meaux'
'Rose de Rescht' see 'De
 Rescht'
rose sickness 21
'Roseraie de l'Haÿ' 165–6
roses, classification of
 12–19; climbing, training
 of 25–8; cultivation of
 20–8; diseases 22; feeding
 21–22; history of 10–12;
 planting 20–21; pruning
 21,22–25; use in the
 garden 28–35
'Russelliana' 234

'Sacramento Rose' see *R.
    stellata mirifica*
'Salet' 166–7
'Sanders' White Rambler'
    235
'Scarlet Fire' see
    'Scharlachglut'
'Scarlet Sweetbriar' see 'La
    Belle Distinguée'
'Scharlachglut' 167–8
'Schneewittchen' see
    'Iceberg'
'Schneezwerg' 168–9
'Seagull' 236–7
'Sombreuil, Climbing' 237–8
'Soupert et Notting' 169–70
'Souvenir de la Malmaison,
    Climbing' 238
'Souvenir de Philémon
    Cochet' 49
'Souvenir du Docteur
    Jamain' 238–40
Species roses 19
'Stanwell Perpetual' 170–1
'Surpasse Tout' 172–3

Tea roses 19
'The Countryman' 173–4
'Tipo Ideale' see *R. ×
    odorata* 'Mutabilis'
'Tricolore de Flandre' 174–6
'Tuscany Superb' 176–7

'Variegata di Bologna' 177–8

'White Pet' 179–80
White rose of York, see *R. ×
    alba* 'Alba Maxima'
'William Lobb' 180–1
'Winchester Cathedral'
    181–2
'Wolley–Dod' 178–9

'Zéphirine Drouhin' 240–1
'Zigeunerknabe' 183